BURRAGE
on
VEGETABLES

ALBERT C. BURRAGE

BURRAGE
on
VEGETABLES

SECOND
EDITION

Revised and Updated by
SUSAN A. HOLLANDER
and TIMOTHY K. HOLLANDER

BOSTON
HOUGHTON MIFFLIN COMPANY
1975

Illustrations by John V. Morris.
Charts by 760 Associates

Library of Congress Cataloging in Publication Data
Burrage, Albert Cameron, 1886–
  Burrage on vegetables.

  Includes index.
    1. Vegetable gardening—United States. I. Hollander, Susan A.
II. Hollander, Timothy K. III. Title.
SB321.B973 1975   635   75-4732
ISBN 0-395-20507-7

Printed in the United States of America

c   10   9   8   7   6   5   4   3   2   1

Preface

OUR INVOLVEMENT with *Burrage on Vegetables* began on Christmas Day in 1968, the winter before our first vegetable garden. The influence of the original version, first published in 1954, on that garden and every one we have had since, has been significant. So far as possible, we faithfully adhered to the Burrage method, although our approach has been somewhat less sophisticated and our experience more limited. Our results, nonetheless, have been rewarding, and it is for this reason that the revised version does not represent a substantive alteration of the original text. Our purpose in undertaking the revision was, for the most part, to help renew a concept of vegetable gardening outmoded by changes that have occurred over the past two decades. As anyone familiar with the original book will see, there has been a conscious effort to retain as much of it as possible. However, there have been some important additions and changes.

The seed list, a feature rarely found in more generalized gardening books, has been brought up to date. We have included sources for most of the varieties Albert Burrage has determined, through years of testing, to be the very best. We have also listed varieties developed more recently that we have found to be of excellent quality.

A great deal of change has taken place in the fields of insecticides, fungicides, and herbicides. For example, DDT was the most valuable deterrent to destructive and troublesome pests twenty years ago. Of course, it is no longer legally available to the home vegetable gardener in our part of the world, but there are several other chemicals equally effective and far safer to use. Organic gardening has received wide acclaim and publicity in recent years; though we subscribe to some of the methods, we are not totally committed to the theory. Our efforts toward eradicating destructive insects through companion planting have met with dismal failure. The careful, but thorough, use of insecticides is essential to the well-being of our garden.

Although the original book was designed for experienced gardeners, we have included information on the basics of growing vegetables from seed, planting in the open garden, and maintenance, a job often neglected by today's gardeners. Albert Burrage taught us the importance of the vegetable garden as a thing of beauty, as an attractive and integral part of the landscape. A well-kept, weedless, and insect-free garden produces superior vegetables and becomes lovely to look at. There is little value in growing mediocre vegetables in a sloppy fashion.

We think there is a strong resemblance between many vegetable gardeners today and their counterparts who grew their own vegetables in Victory gardens during World War II. There are food shortages at the present time that are similar in many respects to those in the 1940s, and it seems likely that these will continue for some time to come. It is our experience that the procurement of top quality, fresh vegetables is both difficult and expensive, and while this is an important part of our reason for growing our own vegetables, our prime intent over the past six years has been to produce and enjoy the very best quality vegetables possible. To be able to by-pass the so-called "fresh" and frozen vegetable sections in the supermarket both winter and summer, knowing that we are eating better vegetables, is most satisfying. It seems incredible to us that the diet of many Americans who are able to have vegetable gardens of their own includes corn on the cob fit only for cattle fodder and tomatoes about as appetizing as the vines on which they were grown.

If your goal is to beat the inflationary spiral in food prices by raising your own vegetables, you may be rewarded. Our experience has been a better than break-even proposition. Although there are one-time expenses, such as fencing, hand tools, freezing and canning equipment, and perhaps a small garden tractor, as well as the annual outlays for seeds, fertilizer, and insecticides, we believe it is possible to effect an economy in the budget, if the garden is large enough to supply vegetables for your family both summer and winter.

We are not weekend gardeners; we devote a considerable amount of time to this endeavor. The planning, planting, maintaining, harvesting, and freezing have become an important part of our lives. Far from being an unpleasant chore, it is a challenge and an immensely rewarding pleasure. We consider Albert Burrage responsible for enriching both our lives and those of our healthy, hungry children.

SUSAN A. HOLLANDER
TIMOTHY K. HOLLANDER

Craigston

Contents

PART THREE

Introduction

WHEN I THINK of all the trash, in the way of home-grown vegetables, that I used to eat, it makes me shudder. Of course, I am interested in planning the garden, in watching the vegetables and fruits grow, and in seeing the improvements made each year. However, what really interests me most is eating the results, for there is nothing like home-grown vegetables and fruits.

Wines coming from two vineyards fifty feet apart can be of entirely different quality; one can be of such fineness that it commands premium prices the world over, and the other can be sold only as an ordinary wine. Two varieties of a particular vegetable can differ in much the same way.

Some of the varieties, which have been selected after years of testing, are little known; a few should be used only when they are half grown; others should be grown only in hotframes, and still others only in coldframes. Until you have eaten these wonderful delicacies, you cannot believe that they actually exist.

You might think that it would be very difficult to raise them. That, fortunately, is not so — these choice vegetables are just as easy, or easier, to raise than the standard, poorer varieties. Carefully selected varieties are a far cry from many of those sold in the markets, which have been raised on 100-acre lots, picked green, and shipped in railroad cars or trucks that take several days in transit.

This is definitely not a book on "how to grow all vegetables." It started simply from my own notes about vegetables in my own garden — what I did and why. Although I had raised vegetables for years, there was no fun in it. The quality was poor, the yield was poor, and, therefore, the cost was high. Then, too, the garden was too far from the house. Most important of all, there was no uninterrupted supply of fresh and tender young vegetables. We generally had a large crop of one variety of rather doubtful virtue maturing at one time, with the result that the quality, or what passed for such, diminished rapidly as the crop grew old. Finally, a clean sweep was made, and the present garden was started in 1929.

At the outset, if you make up your own mind just what your interest is in your garden or proposed garden, you will avoid confusion later. Is the garden merely to supply food as easily and cheaply as possible, or is it to provide vegetables of superb taste and texture that just cannot be bought in the market? In other words, is your interest in quantity or quality? If it is in quantity and the garden is mainly to provide food, then you will be better off buying vegetables at the market, for you will save money and trouble. If your desire is for those superb vegetables that make your mouth water, then by all means have a garden.

Although this is not a cookbook, nevertheless it is a book that has to do with quality, taste, and texture. It has been written from this point of view, and yet I am also interested in how to grow the most with the least amount of work. But if there is a choice between efficiency and quality, then the latter wins.

In writing this book originally, I endeavored to do the following:

First, answer the questions I asked when I first began a vegetable garden. They were: "What varieties to plant and why? From whom to buy the seeds? How big to make the garden? On what dates to plant? What fertilizers to use? What plan to follow? In a way, these notes are merely like recipes in a cookbook. There are many ways to do certain things, and ways perhaps better than those described here, but these are what I use, and, at least, they work well in our home garden at Candlewood in Ipswich, Massachusetts.

Second, stimulate interest in producing vegetables of high

quality. No matter how small the garden, or whether there is a gardener, the suggestions made in the book can be utilized; they will apply regardless of the size of the garden. I feel certain that vegetables of topnotch quality cannot be raised just by following a blueprint. Actual experience is necessary, but I feel equally certain that quality can be improved by a desire to experiment.

Third, provide a definite plan for a garden that will supply vegetables and fruits on an efficient basis. This plan with yearly minor changes has been followed at Candlewood since 1930 and is, therefore, time-tested.

Fourth, reduce expense and the raising of needless substandard or surplus vegetables.

Fifth, show how easy it is to raise vegetables of the very highest quality.

Most of the vegetables sold at average shops would not be graded better than fair, and a great many would be graded poor. Even the very best restaurants hardly ever serve vegetables better than good. So often, big size is taken as an indication of high quality, which is solely a matter of taste and texture. I doubt if one person in a thousand is interested enough to make a real effort to raise or buy first-class vegetables. If this were not so, it would be hard to explain the sale of the horrible vegetables that are used every day, which is such a pity when good vegetables can be grown easily.

The garden I describe is part of our own Candlewood Farm in Ipswich, about three miles from the Atlantic Ocean with an elevation of about fifty feet. In winter, the ground remains frozen, and in summer the days are hot but the nights are cool. Because the garden's so close to the sea, it receives more moisture than if it were even a few miles farther inland. Since the prevailing winds are not from the sea, the growing seasons of plants are not influenced by the cold water. Candlewood used to be a commercial seed farm in the early days, and it has deep and rich soil on top of sand with excellent drainage. On the slope to the east, we can grow very early vegetables. Being on a slight ridge, where there is movement of air, the garden escapes the early and late frosts, which is a factor of considerable value.

Candlewood Farm has been a farm for 310 years and was first owned by Thomas Low in 1641. Its name is derived from the part of Ipswich that was called Candlewood by the early settlers, because they lighted their houses with thin strips of pitch pine from the pine forest that originally covered this section of Ipswich.

Our aim in developing the place has been to gain simplicity and ease of upkeep and to have the gardens and other features as near the house as possible so that they might be constantly enjoyed. The vegetable garden, which has received more attention than anything else, is the result of intensive study and experimentation, with quality rather than quantity as the goal.

One criticism of our garden might be that too much importance is placed on the best tasting vegetables, regardless of cost. My answer to that is summed up in the following points.

1. The cost of the finest seeds is only a little above the cost of the cheapest.

2. To produce the amount of vegetables desired, the area of this garden is very small in comparison with similar gardens at nearby places. It is better to have a small and efficient garden and try to produce the best, rather than a haphazard garden producing a larger crop of poor vegetables.

3. The cost of raising the best vegetables is no more than the cost of raising poor vegetables.

Everyone who has a vegetable garden should draw up his own specifications and make his own plans to fit his needs and tastes. No one garden plan can be presented that will fit all situations. Therefore, consider carefully what you may need and make your plan before you do actual garden work.

The Candlewood garden is 140 by 76 feet, exclusive of walks. It requires the full-time work of one man, with nothing else to do, from March 1 until December 1. During December, January, and February, the gardener can do odd jobs on the place, such as pruning the trees, painting the garden furniture, and other chores.

The market value of the vegetables raised is about equal to the gardener's wages. However, if you did not have a garden, you would not buy all the vegetables this garden will raise. So if costs are vital, it would be better to have a smaller garden or else share the labor with a neighbor.

Inasmuch as a garden of the size described requires the use of a gardener, and the primary object was and is to produce the highest quality vegetables, there was no necessity to crowd the vegetables together or to limit the selection of the varieties. Each vegetable selected was the one that would produce the best results. The distance between rows was that which would be best for hand cultivation and would give the necessary amount of light.

ALBERT C. BURRAGE

Candlewood Farm

Part One

This part has to do with the reasons for having a garden designed to produce only the best tasting vegetables and how to rate the vegetables.

The garden plan is intended to provide a continuous succession of tender young vegetables of the highest quality, regardless of the size of the garden.

We have also included a discussion of our planting techniques, coldframes, and compost.

Vegetables of Quality

CERTAINLY there is not the same pleasure in eating all varieties of vegetables. If you were given your choice of corn, turnips, or spinach, there is not much doubt which one you would select. Everyone should grow only his own favorites and not bother with the rest. To amuse themselves, the Burrages made what is called "The Candlewood Rating Table" for the vegetables they grew.

This table roughly grades the quality of the various kinds of vegetables under different conditions, and by quality is meant only the taste and pleasure of eating. Size does not enter into the matter of quality. It is generally true that the best tasting vegetables are medium in size and normal in appearance. Big ones are generally coarse in texture and tasteless.

The vegetable rating table that follows provokes endless discussion at Candlewood. Your own rating table will do the same in your house. If you can make up a table that will satisfy yourself, you had better call it a day, for it will never satisfy anyone else.

A table like the one on page 4 represents simply personal opinion, and no two people are going to agree on the relative merits of the vegetables. It is interesting to note the divergence of opinion among friends. At Candlewood, the favorites are asparagus, corn, string beans, and peas. However, a friend says she prefers lettuce above all vegetables or fruits, and another says that browned potatoes, which accompany roast beef, is her favorite. So there you are. Before planning a garden, be sure to make up your own rating chart of vegetables.

CANDLEWOOD RATING TABLE (0 TO 100)

Vegetable	Grown at Candlewood	Best veg. stores, summer & fall	Best veg. stores, winter	Chain stores, summer & fall	Chain stores, winter
Asparagus	100	70		70	
Corn	97	70		30	
Peas	95	80	30	70	20
Beans	95	70	30	60	20
Limas	85	70	50	30	25
Baby beets	80				
Baby potatoes	80				
Baby cauliflower	75				
Lettuce	70	50	40	20	10
Celery	70	60	60	40	30
Baby carrots	70				
Baby onions	60				
Brussels sprouts	40	35	35	35	35
Eggplant	30	20	20	20	20
Spinach	30	25	10	25	10
Tomatoes	30	20	5	15	5
Cucumbers	20	20	15	20	15
Parsnips	20	20	20	20	20
Squash	20	15	15	15	15
Potatoes	10	10	10	10	10
Onions	10	10	10	10	10

The ability to distinguish the difference in quality is an acquired art. It is of no great importance, but at least it is a lot of fun. If you once get interested, then no matter where you are, in whatever part of the world, you will immediately start comparing the vegetables to those you know at home.

If someone recommends a vegetable to you, consider a moment before deciding to try it. What are the qualifications of the person giving the advice? Unless he is qualified, the chances are nine out of ten that the variety recommended, if tried, will prove to be of no importance and the experiment will be a waste of time and energy. If a certain variety is best for the farmer because of its shipping qualities, its yield, and other factors, it does not mean that it is best for you.

Every home gardener has to make up his own list of vegetables for his own land, and that is something that can't be done unless one tries several varieties, and then selects the best. When you try a new variety, grow only a half row the first time. If it is better than what you have been growing, then make it one-half of the crop next year. If what you are already growing is fairly good, it is better to be certain of the new variety before taking a chance on something you don't know about.

Although the varieties finally selected for the garden in Ipswich were best for that garden, they won't necessarily be best for gardens in other localities and with different conditions. Most likely, they would do well enough to be rated as good in almost any garden, but, in all probability, at least some others can be found that will do better. To compare two varieties, you should cook and eat them the same way at the same time, but remember that if you obtain from some friend a sample of a variety that tastes better than yours, you can't be certain that it will also be better when it is grown in your own garden. The only way to determine whether some variety is superior to what you have is to grow it in your own garden. We have often had as many as four varieties of one vegetable to compare at one meal. Before you determine that some new variety actually being grown in your own garden is better than your standard variety, make the eating test several times during the growing season. Remember that some varieties are best early in the season and others late in the season. Then, too, certain varieties mature early and won't mature late and vice versa. This is particularly true of peas, raspberries, and strawberries. It takes time and trouble to work out your own selection, but it is well worthwhile once you have done it.

Making the Garden Plan

LOCATION

Few garden locations are perfect. Many garden sites are chosen thoughtlessly even though it is important to choose the best site available. Often it is necessary to select a second-best spot, because there may be trees that would have to be cut down if the best site were used. It is better to have a reasonably satisfactory location than not to have a garden at all, but it is useless to try to have a garden in a place where there is much shade, swamp, ledge, or roots.

Full Sunshine

The garden site should have full sunshine. This cannot be emphasized too much. In the summer the sun rises somewhat north of east. It is, therefore, important to have no tall trees on the northeast side of the garden. This may not seem important in the summer, with its bright sunshine and long days, but certain plants, such as late corn and everbearing raspberries, simply will not ripen if full sun is denied them. Also, keep in mind that large trees have extensive root systems that will interfere with the garden.

Good Soil

This is almost as important as full sunshine. Swampland can be drained; roots can be removed; sand can be enriched with humus — but all at great expense. It is worth sacrificing some of your shrubs or lawn, perhaps even a tree, if you can obtain a good location with good soil.

The ideal soil for growing most vegetables is loam, a soil in which the light and heavy properties are in equal proportions. A soil that is mostly clay will provide poor drainage and poor aeration; a soil that is too sandy will dry out quickly and lose nutrients through the leaching process. Faulty soil structure of either extreme can be corrected by the addition of humus, manure, compost, or peat moss.

The ideal site needs to have two soil conditions; one part of the garden needs good soil with sand beneath to grow early vegetables, and the other part of the garden requires good soil with a subsoil of cold, wet clay, which provides the ideal condition for celery and fall peas. This combination, admittedly, is almost impossible, but if you have one or the other, make the best of what you have. If you cannot have early peas, then try for the other end of the rainbow, which is just as good. In other words, find out the good points of your own soil and then utilize them.

If your garden is located over sand, which is ideal for early vegetables, you will need considerable humus for the best results, and you will also need a sprinkler system, because the sand foundation absorbs rain very quickly. With this foundation, you will find that it pays to use a mulch to retain the soil moisture.

Proximity to the House

Convenience is very important. You will find that you visit the garden often to make plans for the future and to pick and sample the fruits and vegetables. If your garden is too far away, you won't enjoy it because the effort to visit it is too great. Nothing gives more pleasure than picking and eating on the spot a bright red strawberry, young peas right out of the pod, or sweet raspberries off the vine. Until you have experienced the pleasures of walking in your own garden before breakfast, smelling the soil, which is so earthy on a spring morning, and sampling your produce, you will never feel properly close to the soil or fond of your garden.

A well-kept garden is an attractive addition to any landscape. The garden should be near the house so that both you and your guests will have the pleasure of looking at it often. It can be an integral part of landscaping plans, and can readily enhance the attractiveness of your yard.

Various things can be done to make the garden attractive, such as enclosing it in a hedge, having grass walks with strategically placed seats around the borders (inside the hedge), and grass walks through the garden. Low trees on the north make a good windbreak. Pipes and stakes used in the garden can be painted green.

Protection from Frost

For early and late vegetables, a location free from early and late frost is essential. Generally, in any particular locality the crests of the slopes have a longer season free from frost than do the valleys. At Candlewood, the garden is near a crest on an eastern slope, and has a season of 151 days free from frost. An experimental garden, 500 feet away on bottom land on the western side of the crest, has a season of only 124 days. This alone shows the importance of the proper location. If you have any choice in the selection of the proper site, you should inspect the site in the early morning in both the spring and fall to determine the comparative dates when the ground is first fit to plant (thawed, partly dried, and warmed), as well as the last and the first frosts.

Protection from Winds

The better protection a garden has, the better it does. Probably a brick wall around the garden gives the best results, but that is an expensive luxury. A hedge is satisfactory and makes a great deal of difference. It is not only practical, but it is also attractive, provided that it is low enough to permit viewing from a short distance and high enough to be of use. Protect your garden from the cold winds if you can.

Slope

Clearly, the slope of the land must not be so steep as to accelerate the erosion process. Planting rows across rather than up and down the slope reduces, to some degree, the washing away of topsoil; the less slope, however, the better.

SIZE

Obviously, the amount of space available is the key determinant of size. In considering the size of a prospective garden, one must determine the purpose. How many mouths are to be fed? Are the vegetables for immediate eating, or will the freezer be filled for the winter? Another important consideration is the limitation of maintenance time. No garden will produce well unless it is properly cared for; therefore, do not overextend yourself by planting more than you are able to maintain.

The Craigston garden was 210 feet long, with an average width of about 60 feet. We found this size far larger than we needed and ended up with mounds of the more plentiful varieties (tomatoes, zucchini, summer squash, and beans). After several years, we decided our labor should be spent on supplying only the amount of vegetables necessary to feed five mouths all year round, and the size was diminished considerably. As a result of that decision, we gained sufficient space to rotate crops. This book focuses on the garden at Candlewood (140 x 76 feet), which is described in greater detail under "The Garden Plan." In our opinion, this is the optimum size.

WHAT TO GROW

Each owner must decide for himself what he wants to eat and when. Therefore, each garden will be different. It is wise to choose vegetables that adapt well to your conditions — your soil, the length of your growing season, and the amount of time you are able to spend on maintenance.

A number of vegetables are not grown at Candlewood: celtuce, chard, kale, kohlrabi, summer squash, pole and wax beans. It is hard for us to understand anyone's wanting to eat these as long as it is possible to get better vegetables; that, however, is a matter of personal taste and every individual will have his own preferences. In fact, one of the greatest pleasures of gardening is that you can do just as you want and hardly an eyebrow will be lifted, which can't be said about a lot of things in life.

The seasons for vegetables can be divided into three: spring and summer, fall, and winter. The spring and summer season begins with asparagus about May 1 and ends at Candlewood with the first heavy frost, about October 10, which instantly kills the corn, tomatoes, and limas. The moment the first heavy frost arrives, the summer vegetables still standing should be pulled up and discarded in the compost. Otherwise, the garden will look disreputable. The month of July is the important one. Not only should you plan to raise all you want of the kinds you most enjoy, but you should also plan to raise enough extra in that month for freezing and processing.

At the first heavy frost, the fall season begins. Most people think that the first frost marks the end of the garden, but that is far from true. A whole new season begins. The following vegetables can be used daily from the garden for some time, and some are better for the frost: beets, carrots, celery, broccoli, Brussels sprouts, fennel, Jerusalem artichokes, parsnips, and winter squash.

Some of these vegetables should not be used until the frost, since that is when they arrive at their best quality. Then they are delicious. How much better it is to have a whole new garden to look forward to than to eat these vegetables ahead of time, when their quality is not of the best and when the summer vegetables are still excellent. In addition, beans and lettuce can be grown in the coldframe, so, all in all, the fall season is still full of culinary joys.

The winter season for vegetables is probably a good change, for, if home-grown vegetables of the highest quality were available the year round, they would lose some of their charm and interest. For winter consumption vegetables can be grouped into four classes:

1. Those that are generally sold in the markets and are of good quality: Brussels sprouts, broccoli, cabbage, cauliflower. Others of somewhat lesser quality are carrots, celery, lettuce.

2. Those that can be grown in your own garden and stored in a cold cellar, such as winter squash, onions, Jerusalem artichokes, and potatoes; or left in the ground, such as celery and parsnips.

3. Those that can be processed: carrots and beets.

4. Those that can be frozen: asparagus, corn, broccoli, peas, lima beans, green beans, spinach, and tomatoes in the form of sauce to be used for cooking or in the form of thick soup for a cold winter day.

The following outline shows how the vegetables are grouped and how many times we use them. Naturally every family will use different amounts but this table will at least visualize the situation.

Class I. The favorites

Asparagus or beans — One used every day, May 1–Oct. 10
Peas or corn or limas — One used every day, June 6–Oct. 10

Class II.

Baby beets
Baby carrots
Baby onions
Baby potatoes — Two used every day, June 15–Oct. 10
Eggplant
Spinach

Class III. Salad vegetables

Lettuce
Cress
Bunching onions or shallots — Used every day, May 1–Oct. 31
Tarragon

Vegetable	April	May	June	July	Aug.	Sept.	Oct.	Nov.	Dec.
Parsnips									
Lettuce		Hot frame			Garden			Cold frame	
Asparagus									
Spinach		Hot frame			Garden				
Beets			Hot frame		Garden				
Cauliflower					Garden				
Onions					Garden				
Peas			Cold frame	Garden					
Carrots									
Baby potatoes									
Beans				Cold frame					
Corn									
Tomatoes									
Cucumbers									
Eggplant									
Limas									
Brussels sprouts									
Celery									
Squash									

CANDLEWOOD CHART OF PICKING DATES

This chart shows in what periods each vegetable can be available so that you can plan your garden to fit your requirements.

The chart opposite shows the months in which the various vegetables can be picked at Candlewood. Naturally, if your garden is to produce vegetables for consumption only in the summer months, there are some vegetables that need not be grown. But if you want vegetables for as long a season as possible, the chart shows what can be done.

THE GARDEN PLAN

There is no sense in eating old and tough vegetables. It is necessary, therefore, to make a number of plantings if you want a continuous supply of fresh, young vegetables. What is generally not known is the exact number of plantings to make. Most gardeners have nowhere near the necessary number. From the many experiments we have made, we have found that, in order to have a continuous supply of fresh, young vegetables, it is best to have the garden 110 feet long, excluding the asparagus bed, which is permanent. Most gardens are shorter than this, and most gardens attempt to compensate by having longer rows than are desirable. If you use long rows, you produce too much at one time, and nothing is more disappointing than to come home expecting some delicious corn for dinner and find it so old and tough that even the local raccoons are offended. You can overcome the long row problem by planting one-half or one-quarter of a row at a time, but this method makes it difficult to lay out the garden according to a plan and difficult to keep written records. Nevertheless, it is entirely satisfactory for the less serious-minded gardener or for the gardener who does not have available the properly shaped space.

To brighten up a dreary winter weekend, make a diagram of your future garden. We make our plan on stiff cardboard or plywood and cover it with cellophane for protection when we take it to the garden for each planting session. The plan should be simple and the schedule definite. For the rows to get the maximum amount of sunlight, they should run north and south. It is necessary to plan to rotate your crops; some plants take large

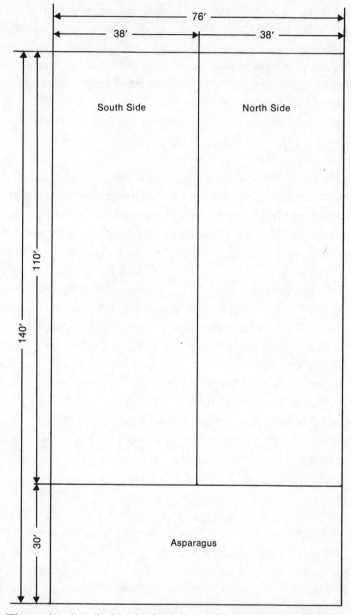

The garden described in this book is 140 feet long and 76 feet wide. It is divided into an area for asparagus and two other areas. Whatever vegetables are grown in one area are the next year grown in the other area.

amounts of certain nutrients out of the soil. A simple way to obtain rotation is to divide the garden in half. What is grown one year in one half is grown the next year in the other half.

The various plantings of each variety of vegetable should be grown side by side insofar as possible. In that way, each group can receive any special treatment that may be necessary, such as watering or spraying. The rows should be planted as close together as possible and still not crowd each other out. Any greater distance between them merely means that there will be a greater area to weed. Some gardeners find a garden tractor useful for cultivating between the rows, in which case the distance between the rows will be determined by the width of the tractor.

For example, we use the following distance between rows:

Celery beds	4 feet
Peas	3 feet
Corn	3 feet
Beans	2 feet
Potatoes	2 feet
Beets	1 foot
Carrots	1 foot
Lettuce	1 foot
Onions	1 foot

Make sure your design will use the land as productively as possible; that is, an early crop should be followed by a late planting. The early peas can be followed by planting strawberries for next year's bed; the late peas can be followed by late plantings of corn; the early spinach can be followed by the Brussels sprouts, which take up considerable room when fully grown; and the early beans can be followed by the late ones. If the garden is on a slope, the earliest crops, such as peas, corn, beets, and onions, should be planted on the highest ground, and the celery on the lowest.

North Side of Garden
First Crop

Garden planting chart — "North Side of Garden / First Crop" with "Followed by" section.

Width	Start Greenhouse Expect	Start Greenhouse Actual	Plant Garden Expect	Plant Garden Actual	Name	MK	Bear Expect Begin	Bear Expect Finish	Bear Actual Begin	Bear Actual Finish	Notes	Followed by
1	Feb 20		Apr 1		Lettuce	MK	June 1	June 14				Beans — Aug 8 / T Oct 10 / T Oct 18
1	"		" 22		Corn	S60	July 17	July 23				" — 8 / 10 / 18
2½			" 22		"	S60	" 17	" 23				14 / 20 / 30
1½											6' Cold Frame	
2			Mar 29		Peas	VF	June 26	July 3			Freeze	Strawberries — Aug 1
3			" 29		"	VF	" 26	" 3				" — " 1
3			" 29		"	VF	" 26	" 33				
3			May 1		Potatoes	IC	" 20	" 12				" — " 1
2			" 18		"		July 12	Aug 1				" — " 1
2			Apr 15		"	RQ	June 18	" 1				
1			" 15		Beets	N	" 22	" 1				
1			May 1		Carrots	RQ	" 28	" 1				
1			" 1		Beets	"	" 28	" 1				
1			" 1		"	N	" 28	" 1				
1			" 1		Carrots	N	July 5	" 1				
1			" 1		"	N	" 5	" 1				
1			" 1		"	RQ	" 5	" 1				
1			" 9		Beets	N	" 7	Sept 1				
1			June 10		Carrots	RB	Aug 1	Dec 1				
1			" 7		Beets	RB	" 1	" 1				
1			" 27		"	N	" 23	Oct 15				
1			July 8		Carrots	RB	Sept 1	Dec 1				
1			" 9		Beets	N	" 15	" 1				
3			" 16		Carrots	S60	" 15	July 28				
3			May 1		Corn	S & G	July 23	Aug 5				
			" 15		"		" 28					

21'

38'

Garden planting plan (oriented with top of page toward West).

Compass: N (up), W–E (horizontal), S (down)

Corn / S60 block

July 3	Corn	S60	Sept 23	Sept 30
": 3	"	S60	": 23	": 30
": 8	"	S60	": 30	To Frost
": 11	"	S60	Oct 4	To Frost

Main garden grid

Width	Sowing date	Crop	Var.			
3	May 27	:	SC	": 19	": 26	Freeze
3	": 27	:	SC	": 19	": 26	
3	June 8	:	SC	": 26	Sept 2	
3	": 17	:	SC	Sept 2	": 9	
3	Mar 29	Peas	WR	June 17	June 24	
3	": 29	:	VF	": 26	July 3	
3	Apr 21	:	L	July 1	": 5	
3	May 6	:	L	": 6	": 11	
3	": 14	:	L	": 12	": 17	
3	": 18	:	L	": 18	": 24	
3	Apr 1	Parsnips	AA	Oct 15	May 1	
2	Feb 20 / May 1	Leeks	M	July 15	Nov 1	
1	": 20 / ": 1		M	": 15		
2	Apr 1	Cauliflower	PH	July 1	Aug 1	
2	May 8	:	PH	": 20	": 10	
2	": 24	:	PH	Aug 10	Sept 10	
2	June 4	:	PH	Sept 1	": 20	
8	May 1	½ Row Cucumbers	M	July 18	Oct 10	
8	June 1	½ Row Squash	GD	Oct 10	Oct 10	

Dimensions: 62', 80', 110', 38'

South Side of Garden - First Crop

	Start Greenhouse Expect	Actual	Plant Garden Expect	Actual	Name	Bear Expect Begin	Finish	Bear Actual Begin	Finish	6' Cold Frame	Followed by Begin	Followed by			
1½	Mar 18				Peas A	June 6	June 15				June 24	Corn	SC	Sept 9	Sept 18
3			:: 18		:: A	:: 6	:: 15				:: 28	::	SC	:: 16	:: 22
1½															
3					Strawberries	June 11	July 9								
3½					::	:: 11	:: 2								
3½					::	:: 17	:: 6								
3½					::	:: 21	:: 10								
2½			Apr 1		Spinach A	May 21	June 10								
1			:: 1		:: ::	:: 21	:: 10								
1			:: 10		:: ::	June 1	:: 20								
1			:: 10		:: ::	:: 1	:: 20								
1			:: 10		Onions Shallot A	:: 1	:: 20				June 20	Brussels Sprouts	C	Oct 17	Dec 15
1			:: 10		:: ::	July 15	Sept 1								
1			:: 10		:: ::	:: 15	:: 1								
1			:: 10		:: ::	:: 15	:: 1								
1	Feb 20		May 1		:: DYG	:: 15	:: 10								
1	:: 20		:: 1		:: DYG	:: 15	:: 10								
1	:: 20		:: 1		:: DYG	:: 15	:: 10								
1	:: 20		:: 1		:: DYG	:: 15	:: 10								
1	:: 20		:: 1		:: WQ	Aug 1	Sept 1				July 5	Lettuce	B		Schedule
1	Apr 5		June 10		:: WQ	Aug 5	:: 1					::	::		
1			See Sched		Radish C										
1			::		Onion JB										
1			::		Lettuce WB										
1			::		::										
1			::		::										
2			Apr 15		Beans T	July 1	July 10				July 24	Beans	T	Sept 11	Sept 22
2			May 12		::	:: 7	:: 18				Aug 1	::	::	:: 22	Oct 3
											7	::	::	:: 30	:: 10

Dimensions at left margin: 22', 37', 45'

N
W E
S

Aug 9	" 20	31					
	" 20	" 31				July 5	25
	" 31	Sept 11				14	
Potatoes GM Sept 1	Sept 15					May 1	
GM	" 1	" 15				" 1	
Limas F242 Aug 10	Oct 10					June 1	
" 10	" 10					" 1	
" 10	" 10					" 1	
" 10	" 10					" 1	
" 10	" 10					" 1	
" 10	" 10					" 1	
Celery TFH Oct 10	Nov 1		Mar 15			" 1	
TFH " 10	" 1		" 15			" 1	
TFH " 10	" 1		" 15			" 1	
TFH " 10	" 1		" 15			" 1	
" 10	Dec 1		" 15			" 1	
" 10	" 1		" 15			" 1	
" 10	" 1		" 15			" 1	
Fennel F Sept 20	Nov 1					" 6	
" 20	" 1					" 6	
Tomatoes MH July 20	Oct 10		Mar 15			" 1	
Egg ½ Row JK Aug 3	Oct 10		" 1			" 1	
½ Row S. Tomatoes RC Sept 15	Oct 10		" 15			" 12	

110'

38'

Planting

STARTING FLATS INDOORS

A gratifying way to get a jump on spring is to start flats indoors. In our area, the growing season is so short that a few varieties started from seed outdoors will not mature before the first fall frost. Then, too, other varieties mature so late in the season that it is hardly worthwhile to include them in your garden. Tomatoes are an excellent example of the former; peppers and eggplant are examples of the latter. One of our objectives has been to obtain the earliest harvests possible. Although vegetable seedlings may be readily purchased from local roadside stands and commercial greenhouses, starting your own seedlings is both rewarding and economical if it is done in quantity. We found that we were limited in the choice of varieties available at sources nearby, which led to our initial experiments with flats.

This project does not necessarily require a greenhouse, although the latter certainly provides the most ideal conditions. At Craigston, we have had good luck growing seedlings both near our sunny kitchen window and in the cellar under fluorescent lights. We find the following vegetables worth growing from seed: beets, broccoli, Brussels sprouts, cauliflower, celery, cucumbers, eggplant, leeks, lettuce, onions, parsley, peppers, and tomatoes.

The following information pertains to growing seedlings either in a greenhouse, near a window with a southern exposure, or under lights.

Planting Medium

We have learned the hard way that one must use sterile potting soil for starting seeds. In this way only can "damping-off" be avoided. This is a microscopic fungus growth that attacks young seedlings and is caused by contaminated soil. During our first year at Craigston, we used soil from the garden and lost many seedlings because of damping-off. A mixture in equal parts of garden loam, well-rotted compost, peat moss, and coarse sand, which we have used, must be baked in the oven for an hour at 300° in order to kill the fungus. The flats should be treated with either benomyl or captan as additional protection from damping-off. If this seems too messy or too much trouble — and it is — there are packaged starting mediums available commercially that we now find well worth a small-scale investment. Vermiculite and perlite may be added to lighten the mixture. There are probably as many formulas for potting soil as there are gardeners, and each gardener considers his concoction the best. There are, however, several qualities that cannot be ignored. The mixture must be light enough to allow the seedlings to develop strong root growth, porous enough to permit proper drainage (controlled by the addition of sand), and rich enough to provide the necessary nutrients. The texture of the soil is of greater importance than its richness.

Flats

Flats, wooden or plastic containers 3 or 4 inches deep with holes in the bottom for drainage, may be purchased at any garden supply store. Crockery (pieces of broken clay pots) or simply small rocks must be placed over the holes in plastic flats to prevent loss of soil when watered. Wood flats should be lined with newspaper for the same reason. Then the flats may be filled up to half an inch from the top with potting soil. Next, water the flat thoroughly before you sow the seeds, but remember that seeds like moist, not wet, soil. Tiny seeds, like lettuce, should merely be sprinkled over the top and pressed down gently, rather than covered. Medium-sized seeds, like broccoli, may be planted in 2 to 3 rows and covered thinly. Large seeds, such as squash, cucumber, pumpkin, or melon, may be poked in with a finger and covered. As a general rule, the larger the seed, the greater the depth of planting. The larger seeds may also be started in individual peat pots, three or four to a pot. After germination, the weaker seedlings can be snipped with scissors, allowing only the fittest to survive. The flats should be covered with clear plastic wrap and placed in a warm location, out of direct sunlight, to promote strong root growth. The plastic wrap keeps the moisture sealed in so that there is no need to disturb the seeds by watering. If the flats do dry out before germination, spray them gently with a mister. As soon as the seeds germinate, take the covers off and put the flats near a sunny window or under lights (which can be turned off at night). Do not forget to label your flats; tiny plants can be hard for the beginner to recognize. If the seedlings are too thick, as they often are, they must be thinned. We find the best way to thin, without disturbing the delicate root growth, is with a small pair of scissors. When the second pair of leaves appears, it is time to transplant the seedlings to individual peat pots or to other flats where they will have more room to develop. A small spoon is handy for this purpose. At this point, the seedlings have outgrown the need for sterile soil and a more nutritious planting medium, including garden loam and compost, can be used. Choose the healthiest looking plants and treat them very gently. Sometimes, some of the seedlings will look spindly; pinching the tops back slightly will strengthen them. A little plant food can be helpful at this stage, also. The flats or pots must be turned each day to avoid the legginess that develops as the seedlings reach for the sun.

As late spring moves in and the time approaches for setting out the seedlings in the open garden, it is wise to accustom young plants to the harsher conditions they will soon have to endure. Set your flats outdoors on warm and calm days for "hardening off." It is amazing how much damage a breezy spring day can do to young seedlings, so be sure to choose only a sheltered, sunny spot on calm days.

The beginner may want to use seed starter kits, which can be purchased. These are simply flats with seeds and planting medium already prepared. One simply removes the lid and waters the flat. While these are convenient and fun for the person who grows only one or two varieties of vegetables, this method is certainly less rewarding and is hardly economical if you have a garden of any size.

Another modern development, which serves to save a few steps, is the peat pot. This is a small pot made out of compressed peat, which decays in the garden, adding nutrients to the soil. Its use eliminates a transplanting step and the shock of disturbing root growth in that final, important move.

Peat pellets, which resemble Hydrox cookies, may also be used to start seedlings. When soaked in water, they swell up to become a little pot filled with sterile planting medium. Simply plant two or three seeds and later thin to one seedling; then set the whole thing out in the garden. We find these less successful than the peat pots because they are so very small, and they tend to fall over because they haven't flat bottoms.*

SEEDS

This does not purport to be a thorough discussion on the subject of seeds, since there are already volumes available at most public libraries. At the outset it should be noted that we depend solely on the reliable seed houses as a source of supply; it is our opinion that seeds hoarded by the amateur grower from last year's crop generally turn out to be mediocre producers the following year. Unless they are skillfully chosen and meticulously stored in a dry container over the winter, the results can be most disheartening. One of our greatest pleasures has been to peruse the seed catalogs carefully in midwinter, and make the momentous decision on what to order when the ground is still solid with frost and the garden

* An excellent book on this subject is *The Complete Book on Growing Plants from Seed* by Elda Haring, Grandview, Missouri: Diversity Books, 1967.

blanketed with snow. In the late fall, don't forget to write to several different seed houses to obtain their catalogs, which are generally available in January.

The enchantment with saving seeds has led many gardeners to forgo testing a new, improved variety first available the following spring. Also, a number of seeds now available are hybrid strains; that is, a cross between two parents each with desirable and uniform characteristics. The purpose is to obtain, through crossbreeding, traits such as disease resistance, vigor, yield, and quality; yet it is a waste of time to save these seeds since they revert back to one or the other parent strain the following year. Although there are those who take great pride in being self-sufficient in this aspect, we feel it is simply not worth the trouble. The cost of seeds, although not insulated from the effects of inflation, is certainly one of the least expensive components of the home vegetable garden, yet they are the key to a winning crop.

All vegetation does not propagate through seeds, but all seeds, whether of vegetables, flowers, or trees, are similar in one respect: they contain not only the embryonic plant, but also nourishment for early growth. They differ in size from the minuscule lettuce and carrot seeds to the giant blue Hubbard, and come in all shapes, wrinkled and smooth, flat and round. Depending on the variety, they need varying degrees of light, warmth, humidity, and space in order to germinate properly. Seed packets will often contain useful information, such as planting directions, the amount of row required for the contents, and whether the seeds have been treated. Virtually all seedsmen now include the percentage of seeds that, according to their tests, can be expected to germinate.

There are several safe and effective fungicides on the market and available through seed catalogs. These include captan, benomyl, Bordeaux, maneb and red oxide of copper. We use captan, a mild, organic fungicide, since it not only controls damping-off, but also acts as an aid to seed germination. It is available as a 50 percent wettable powder and is also a component of several general purpose sprays, like Ortho Home Orchard Spray, and seed treatments, like

Isotox 25 Seed Treater F. If your seeds are not pretreated by the grower, we think it a good idea to treat them with captan or a mixture that contains it. We use it for beans, beets, corn, muskmelon, peas, tomatoes, and winter squash, and the results are noticeably effective.*

Below is a list of the seed houses, still in existence, that the authors have used. There are many others of equal excellence, although not all of them stock the varieties described. Conditions of soil and climate vary widely throughout the country, and for any given area varieties other than those suggested may well prove better. The practical gardener will experiment before deciding what is best from the point of view of his own taste and his own gardening circumstances.

Joseph Harris Co., Inc., Moreton Farm, Rochester, N.Y. 14624.

W. Atlee Burpee Co., Philadelphia, Pa. 19132.

Robson Seed Farms Corporation, Hall, N.Y. 14463.

Geo. W. Park Seed Co., Inc., Greenwood, South Carolina 29647.

Littlefield, Wyman Co., Abington, Mass.

The Chas. C. Hart Seed Co., Wethersfield, Conn. 06109.

Agway, Box 1333, Syracuse, N.Y. 13201.

W. J. Unwin Ltd., Histon, Cambridge, England.

Chase Seeds Ltd., Benhall, Saxmundham, Suffolk, England.

Seedway, Inc., Hall, N.Y. 14463.

Vilmorin-Andrieux, Service Exportation, 4, quai de la Mégisserie, Boite Postale N° 30–01, Paris, France.

Gurney Seed and Nursery Co., Yankton, S.D. 57078.

---

* Insecticide and pesticide formulations are changing very rapidly. Some recent issues have already changed, or will soon become obsolete, as manufacturers comply with new federal regulations; the deadline for the new formulations is early 1976. The reader should check the label of each pesticide for registration, that is, for the specifications about both insect species and crop, before applying any chemical compound or brand recommended in this book to his vegetables or to his garden soil. One formulation of a given brand may burn the crop; another formulation of the same name may be suitable for ridding the garden of a particular pest and cause no harm to anything but the insect to be destroyed.

COLDFRAMES

The advantages of one or more coldframes adjacent to the vegetable garden are numerous. The uses are first, for starting seeds early in the spring to be transplanted elsewhere in the garden after all danger of frost is past; second, for starting seeds early to be grown to maturity in the coldframe; third, for extending a low crop well into the fall beyond the time when the garden is ordinarily cleaned up for winter. A fourth use is for forcing spring bulbs, such as daffodils. The cover eliminates the chore of digging through deep snow in February to bring the bulbs into the house or greenhouse.

The coldframe is the poor man's greenhouse. Without it, your growing season will be limited by weather; with it, you will be able to start before spring and, later, to produce vegetables well after your neighbor's garden is dormant. Basically, the coldframe is designed to trap the sun's heat, and to afford protection from the cooling and drying effects of the wind.

The construction can be as simple or elaborate as you wish. In its most rudimentary form, it consists of a bottomless box with wooden walls and a glass or clear plastic cover. It may be situated in a permanent location, which is desirable, or it may be portable. The house at Craigston had been remodeled a number of times and there were many unused storm windows about. These are most satisfactory for covers — although a heavy-gauge plastic will do — and their size will dictate the size of the frame.

First, select a location that will be free of shade all day long. In our opinion, the ideal spot is across the end of the garden, so that the frame is oriented directly to the south. There is no need for it to be inside a wire fence since a well-constructed frame should provide adequate protection from marauding rabbits, woodchucks, and the like. Next, dig a pit, the same dimensions as the frame, about 18 inches deep, and refill it with about 6 inches of coarse builder's sand to allow for good drainage. The frame should then be set in at an angle so that the southern end is about 6 inches below the northern end to insure that sunlight reaches all of the seedlings. The soil mixture, described earlier under "Starting Flats Indoors," is then placed in the frame to a depth of about 12 inches. The frame itself, whether constructed of wood or concrete, should be tall enough so that the cover is a minimum of 12 inches above the soil surface at the low end. This will insure that early spring corn does not reach the glass before the frame can be opened permanently to the weather. The cover should be securely and snugly fastened with hinges at the high end and sturdy hooks and eyes at the low end, so that it may be propped open with a stake during sunny days to prevent the seedlings from being burned. If you use wood construction, be sure to treat all surfaces with creosote or copper naphthenate (a brand of the latter is Cuprinol) to prevent it from rotting. The soil in the frame should be thoroughly soaked a day or so before planting, and under no circumstances should it be allowed to dry out. It is wise to treat the soil at this time with Diazinon.

At Candlewood, coldframes are used for growing early corn, lettuce, beets, cauliflower, and peas. After all danger of frost is past, the covers are removed, and the crop is allowed to grow as if there were no frame. Peas can be obtained about eleven days earlier than usual and corn about six days earlier with the use of a coldframe. Since the pea season is relatively short, it seems worthwhile to start at least a portion of the crop in coldframes. Other vegetables, such as lettuce, radishes, beets, broccoli, cauliflower, parsley, and spinach, can be grown with great success, and it is rewarding to experiment on your own.

A hotframe is basically a coldframe heated artificially with either hot-water pipes or electric heating cables embedded in the soil. Coldframes are particularly suited to cool weather crops, and the hotframe is useful for the more sophisticated gardener who wants to start varieties that thrive on warmth, for example, tomatoes, peppers, lettuce, beets, cauliflower, and eggplant.

SOWING SEEDS OUTDOORS

When to Plant

When to plant? That is the question asked by all gardeners, experienced and inexperienced. Every spring is different, every location is different, and every garden has its own peculiarities. Experienced gardeners watch the soil and the trees and shrubs around their property, or use a date established by years of trial and error. The trick is to produce the earliest harvest possible without wasting too many seeds. Both at Craigston and Candlewood, we have planted earlier than the charts recommend and with very happy results. Charts showing the average date of the last killing frost in spring can give you only a general idea of the optimum time to plant. A garden located along the coastal salt marshes will be frost-free before a garden two or three miles inland. Likewise, two locations within several hundred yards of each other and separated by only a few feet of elevation will have different seasons.

One of the great pleasures in having a vegetable garden is to be able to enjoy asparagus, peas, and corn earlier than you expect them. Everyone who has this experience takes a little extra credit for himself and likes to proclaim to all who will listen that "peas have come." When the weather is unseasonably cold, there is a little satisfaction in being able to predict, with reasonable accuracy, that the peas or corn won't mature for at least a given number of days.

It is fairly easy, however, to make these predictions if you keep a list of a few seasonal dates and facts. An example of such a chart follows. If you plan to keep these records, write them on a sheet of paper and hang it in a place where you will see it often. These records will never be kept unless they are frequently in sight. Beside the chart can be posted the list of vegetable maturing dates.

On the seasonal date list (page 29) there is a record for degree days. This was a record kept by the U.S. Weather Bureau to show on what days heating was deemed necessary in apartment buildings,

SEASONAL DATES

		Degree days	
Snow gone	Mar. 12		
Ground thawed	Mar. 12		
March degree days		966	
April average temp. 1–10			44°
Forsythia blossoms	Apr. 17		
Asparagus first cutting	Apr. 28		
Asparagus second cutting	May 1		
April average temp.			46°
April degree days		539	
Degree days total		1505	
Rhubarb	May 4		
Crabapples blossom	May 8		
Lilacs blossom	May 11		
Peas in frame blossom	May 21		
Peas in garden blossom	May 23		
Elms first green	May 23		
May average temp.			57°
May degree days		245	
Degree days total		1750	
Peas in frames bear	June 6		
Peas in garden bear	June 17		
Corn in frames, tassels	June 25		
June degree days		66	
Degree days total		1816	
Corn in garden, tassels	July 1		
Corn in frame, bear	July 17		
Corn in garden, bear	July 23		
First frost	Oct. 1		
Heavy frost	Oct. 10		
Last corn	Oct. 10		
First snow 1 in. deep	Dec. 26		

and it is now widely used. Sixty-five degrees is the standard; if the average temperature of the day was 60 degrees, it would mean that

the day was classified as a 5-degree day. This is reported daily in
the newspapers, and the report made on the first day of each month
shows the total degree days for the preceding month. By taking
the degree days for March, April, and May, one can easily compare
the spring seasons.

If you wish to have the fun of predicting when your vegetables
will mature, keep a record of what happens. The date that shows
when the ground is completely thawed has a great deal to do with
the appearance of the first asparagus. Then, too, the mean
temperature for the first ten days of April also affects the asparagus

PICKING DATES — IPSWICH

Parsnips	Mar.	12
Asparagus first cutting	Apr.	28
Asparagus second cutting	May	1
Lettuce (hotframe)		1
Rhubarb		4
Spinach		21
Beets (hotframe)		21
Lettuce (coldframe)	June	1
Peas (coldframe)		6
Lettuce (garden)		12
Peas		17
Beets		18
New potatoes		20
Carrots		22
Beans	July	1
Corn, Seneca 60 (coldframe)		17
Cucumbers		18
Tomatoes		20
Corn, Seneca 60		23
Corn, Sugar and Gold		28
Eggplant	Aug.	3
Limas, Fordhook 242		10
Corn, Seneca Chief		19

date. Peas bear about three weeks after the blossoms have formed, and corn can be picked about twenty-three days after the tassels have started.

Some vegetables are hardy and can be planted as soon as the frost is out of the ground, or as soon as the soil is workable, that is, dry enough to be plowed. Seedlings of these vegetables will withstand heavy frosts, nights when the temperature falls as low as 28 degrees. Examples of these are peas and spinach. Some vegetables must wait until all the cold weather is past and the soil has warmed up: eggplant, squash, muskmelon, tomatoes, and cucumbers.

Then there is the question of how late one can plant and still produce a harvest before the first fall frost. This depends upon the number of days needed for the vegetable to reach maturity, how much growing heat is needed, and when the first fall frost is expected.

Very careful and voluminous records have been kept at Candlewood, and an ideal planting schedule to obtain young, tender vegetables throughout the summer has been worked out. The planting schedule is based on the date the ground is first workable enough for planting. At Candlewood, that date is March 29, but at Craigston it was found to be several days later. In order to adjust the timetable to suit your locality, use the date when the ground is first workable as a guide to alter the schedule. For most gardeners, it is impossible to follow a schedule as closely as is done at Candlewood. For those unfortunate enough to be away from the garden on weekdays from nine to five, weekends and occasional evenings are the only times available to accomplish the work. There are many things that interfere, and it is important to be able to readjust the schedule. At Craigston, we are limited to weekends and have used the nearest date on the Candlewood timetable as a guide. Although we are forced to endure certain gaps in steady production, we manage to obtain a reasonably balanced harvest. You will not be more than three days off the Candlewood schedule.

Preparation of Soil

This is most important. Seeds need well-pulverized, rockless, clodless soil in which to grow. A new garden is obviously more work to prepare and this job is best begun during October. At Craigston, we had the garden plowed to a depth of 8 to 10 inches by a local farmer ($25 for about one-third of an acre) and then went over it thoroughly to remove heavy clods and rocks. If you live in New England, you will get a thorough lesson in geology. It sometimes seems as if all of the glaciers melted thousands of years ago on the very site you have selected for your garden, and intentionally deposited their ice-borne stones to provide you with the exercise entailed in moving them aside.

When the soil was relatively free of obstacles, we used our Gravely garden tractor with the cultivator attachment to pulverize the soil further. After continuing this procedure both spring and fall for several years, we finally ended up with a proper seed bed. Compost and manure can be churned into the soil in the fall when the ground is easiest to work and when there are fewer pressing outdoor chores. While it is important to pulverize the soil for a new garden, care should be given not to overwork the soil. This leads to crusting after spring rains, which prevents a number of seeds from breaking through the soil's surface.

In the spring, we have the garden plowed by a large tractor, then cultivate, as we go along, only the portion we intend to plant. We use compost and sometimes manure by the shovelful in the rows before we plant. Additionally, at this time the garden is treated with Diazinon.

Garden Layout

The garden should be carefully laid out in a true rectangle with permanent markers. Pieces of galvanized iron pipe, 1 inch in diameter and 18 inches long, driven into the ground until the top is about 3 inches above the soil, are excellent for this purpose. Each corner of the garden and the corners of the permanent asparagus bed should be marked. If you intend to include other perennials, such as raspberries, strawberries, or rhubarb, these areas should also be permanently delineated.

Rows that are not parallel give the garden a sloppy appearance and should be avoided. It is worth taking the little trouble necessary to have the garden look neat and orderly. Both at Craigston and Candlewood, a fence around the garden is essential to keep out rabbits, dogs, and children. Chicken wire comes in a variety of gauges and heights. We have found the 3-foot, square mesh type the easiest to work with, the most durable, and the most aesthetically pleasing. Another advantage is that it is the least likely to sag at the top.

Our installation method is relatively simple and should insure that the process does not have to be repeated every spring. Start by driving a 5-foot iron stake, with hooks on it, at each corner 2 feet into the ground and then weave the end of the wire roll onto the starting point. Using a hoe, dig a shallow trench around the garden, allowing the wire to be about 5 inches below the surface of the ground. This discourages rabbits from sampling the crops. Next, using a sledge hammer, drive in 3-foot metal stakes (available at most hardware stores) every 8 to 12 feet around the garden and

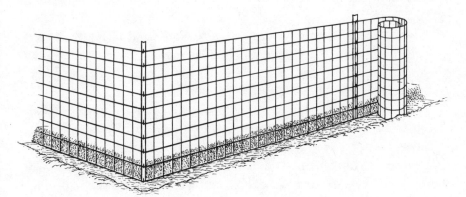

attach the wire to the posts. This is best accomplished by two people, one to pull the wire taut and the other to secure it to the hooks on the stakes. The final step is to hoe the dirt back over the trench in order to cover the bottom of the fence. Wooden stakes (1 x 3 inches), each with a pointed end, may be substituted at regular intervals if the expense of metal stakes becomes prohibitive. They are not, however, nearly as satisfactory. If dogs are a problem, a higher fence is needed. There is nothing more disheartening than watching a dog romp through your garden, destroying tiny seedlings.

Sowing the Seeds

First, if you have children under six, build a sandbox next to the garden outside the fence; children in the garden before germination spell instant disaster. It is wise to plan the night before which seeds are to be planted, and do any reading on the subject then. Most seed packets give excellent directions about how far apart and how deeply the seeds should be planted, how much to cover, and any particular care a certain vegetable may need. Stick to your garden plan and don't feel driven to empty the packet. You will need more seeds for successive plantings and replantings in case cold, wet weather causes poor germination. The sowing of seeds takes patience if it is done by hand. If they are sowed too thickly, the thinning job later is overwhelming and there is much waste. Mechanical seeders are available but seem to us an unnecessary luxury.

Some seeds, such as squash, watermelons, and cucumbers, are planted in hills. Many beginning gardeners have been confused by this term. It is a grouping of seeds, not a mound as the name implies.

Mark your vegetable rows and any plants you are testing. You can make very satisfactory markers by buying stiff, white plastic sheets about $\frac{1}{16}$ inch thick and cutting them into pieces about 3 by 4 inches. You can mark these with a china marking pencil — a crayon-type pencil that is indelible and will withstand sun and rain, but can be cleaned off with gasoline and used again. The markers can be supported by a wire holder. The wire, of a thickness similar to a coat hanger, is cut into 20-inch lengths, and one end is wound on a form, such as a hoe handle, into a tight coil about 1 inch in diameter. If the marker is inserted into this, it will never come loose. Wood label sticks are small, and easily become smudged with soil.

Transplanting

Transplanting young seedlings is a very delicate task. It is best to choose a cloudy or drizzly day to set out seedlings in order to protect them from the shock of heat and light. They should be covered for a few days with boxes or Hotkaps, and it is essential that the root growth not be disturbed. Watering the seedlings an hour or two before setting them out helps to loosen the roots and strengthen the plant. Dig a hole with the trowel, pour water (we often mix it with manure), in the hole, set the plant in, and firm the soil gently around it. Transplanted seedlings need tender loving care, and should not be allowed to dry out.

SOIL AND COMPOST

To maintain the humus content in a vegetable garden, at least four cords of farm manure, horse or cow, are required per acre. To improve the soil and to have a really topflight garden that produces large amounts of the highest quality vegetables, a great deal more is actually needed. In the days of old-fashioned farming, it was not uncommon to use thirty or even sixty cords per acre. Before organic garden compost was used at Candlewood, farm manure at the rate of fourteen cords to the acre was applied. At this rate, the soil is covered with a ½-inch layer of manure. When less than this amount was used, it was found that the soil was harder to work. Consequently, when it was decided to use organic garden compost, the same amount of compost was necessary to maintain the essential humus content of the soil.

In order to compare the results of vegetables grown with manure and those grown with organic garden compost, we grew the following vegetables in each, with all other conditions remaining the same.

Results grown with organic compost	
Celery	Plants double the size
Peas	No difference
Potatoes	Twice the yield
Squash	Twice the yield
Tomatoes	Twice the yield

In all of these tests, holes or trenches were dug and compost was worked into the soil. It is curious that the use of compost under peas produced no improvement. However, the appearance of the other vegetables grown with compost was better; the leaves looked healthier. In fact, the tomatoes retained their foliage much later in the fall and did not dry up. Vines of the squash plants grew far

The celery plant at left was grown on compost; the plant at right was grown on manure.

longer than those without compost, and the fruit was more than twice the size.

The quality of the vegetables was also better; all, except the peas and the squash, tasted better. As far as peas and squash were concerned, no difference was noted. Lettuce, grown on compost, is much more luxuriant in appearance and the heads are slightly larger.

It is not easy to make compost and there isn't much fun in turning a compost pile or feeding it through a shredder. It is very difficult to visualize the amounts of compost required. Farm manure can be bought by the cord, and it is easy in some parts of the country to ask a farmer to send you so many cords. But if you use garden compost, you have to make it yourself, and the figures in regard to the amounts used are interesting.

The following table shows the compost needed per 1000 square feet for given depths of application.

Application	*Cords of compost per acre*	*Inches of compost on soil*	*1 cu. ft. compost will cover (sq. ft.)*	*Cu. ft. compost needed for 1000 sq. ft.*
Maintenance	4	⅛	96	10
Light	7	¼	48	21
Heavy	14	½	24	42
For special purposes	60	2	6	166

Often the recommendation is made to spread organic compost 2 inches deep over the garden. For a garden of only 1000 square feet, a pile or bin 4 x 20 x 4 feet is required for the green compost. Such a quantity is out of all reason, unless you are in a situation (almost unknown these days) where there are unlimited supplies for the compost pile. Luckily such quantities are unnecessary.

This brings up the question: What is the maximum amount of organic compost that can be made easily and economically? Obviously the answer is: All you can make from the available garden refuse, grass clippings, and leaves, plus the necessary amount of farm manure. The garden refuse, leaves, and clippings have to be collected in any event, and it is just as easy to put them on a compost pile as on a dump. If you do make a compost pile, the amount of farm manure required is slightly less than if farm manure alone were used on the garden. This lesser amount of manure about balances the cost of the extra labor in making the compost. The real advantage is that the compost pile produces many more pounds of vegetables (of better quality) than when farm manure alone is used. If you use more compost than what you can make from your garden refuse and grass clippings, you must consider three expensive factors:

First, you have to produce or buy suitable material for composting.

Second, you must use more farm manure.

Third, more labor is involved, but what is your own time worth?

Unless you are very fortunately situated, it is not easy either to raise or to buy suitable compost material. The result is that the cost of the extra compost is very high; in fact, as far as we are concerned, it is prohibitive. Consequently, as much as we would like to use compost more than ½ inch deep on the garden, we have come to the conclusion that this amount is all we can practically provide. Fortunately ½ inch of compost is really a very large amount — the equivalent in volume of fourteen cords of farm manure per acre and probably of thirty cords in value. From our tests, ½ inch of compost is to be preferred to farm manure used alone.

At the rate of fourteen cords per acre this amounts to one-third of a cord of finished compost for every 1000 square feet. To make one-third of a cord of finished compost, one-third of a cord of farm manure is required. To make this amount of compost, a bin of eighty-four cubic feet, or roughly 4 x 5 x 4 feet, is required for every 1000 square feet of garden. If it is not feasible to make one-third of a cord, then at least some should be made — no matter how little. If only a very little can be made, it should be used to the best advantage, a handful to each tomato and eggplant and a little for the celery.

At the rate of fourteen cords of finished compost per acre, four cords per 10,640 square feet were used. These four cords of finished compost were made from four cords of manure and all the garden refuse, grass clippings, and weeds, that we could find.

The size of the bin is 9 x 25 x 5 feet. Since the garden refuse is added to the pile during the entire garden season, there is some shrinkage during the season so that the pile is never 5 feet high.

The weight of the finished compost is fifty pounds per cubic foot or about 25,000 pounds for the four cords. Our manure weighed about forty pounds per cubic foot, so there is no great difference in the weights to be moved.

The following method is used for making compost.

There are two bins, a large one and a small one, built of 2-inch planks, both with removable ends. Into the large bin, 9 x 25 x 5 feet, we put all the garden refuse and grass clippings for the garden season, and make it according to Sir Albert Howard's Indore process. This method consists of spreading 6 inches of garden refuse, weeds, grass clippings, and other plant material; then we add 2 inches of farm manure with a sprinkling of ground limestone and a thin covering of dirt. The corn stalks are kept separate; as soon as there are enough to make the operation worthwhile, they are run through the shredding machine and added to the pile. In this form, they compost much more rapidly.

To obtain thorough composting, we find it necessary to have chimney holes in the compost. If the garden refuse is dry, we apply water, since the compost must be damp. We tried disposing of the kitchen garbage by adding it to the compost pile and came to the conclusion that the amount involved was so small that it was not worth the extra trouble.

By December, the pile shrinks to about 3 feet in depth. The material is not yet fully composted and requires more time to

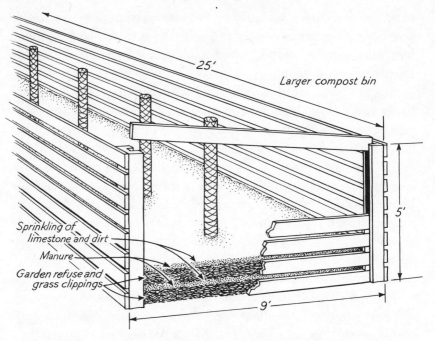

25'

Larger compost bin

5'

Sprinkling of
limestone and dirt

Manure

Garden refuse and
grass clippings

9'

complete the process. To save loss of heat and leaching of valuable fertilizing elements, one-half of the pile is shoveled onto the other so that the pile becomes 9 x 14 x 5 feet. This step makes for a more compact pile that is more easily protected from the weather. The pile is covered with straw, which acts as an insulating material; then corrugated sheet steel or canvas or plastic is laid over the top to keep out the rain and snow. By the first of the following April, the compost process is almost completed.

The compost is then run through a shredding machine. This machine is simply a rapidly revolving shaft, holding a number of blades, that is driven by a small gasoline engine. As the material is fed into the hopper, the revolving blades chop it up into very small particles. The compost that is passed through the shredder is really superb material and the minute size of the particles makes it readily available to the plant roots. In passing through the shredder, the material is blown by the shredder into the second bin, the one that is 9 x 20 x 5 feet. A slight further reaction takes place, evidenced by a rise in temperature. This material is also covered to prevent heat loss and to prevent weeds from growing. It is left in the bin all summer.

We use wooden bins for their numerous advantages, the most important of which is that no time is lost in shaping up the sides of the compost pile. Manure and loam can be dumped beside it so that they are readily available. It is easy to cover the top of the pile with straw, peat moss, or plastic to prevent weeds from growing; finally, the finished compost can be covered with corrugated iron or boards or plastic to prevent loss of nutrients by leaching during the winter. Because the bin has removable ends, the truck can be backed into it to be loaded with a minimum amount of labor. With so much compost to make, it is certainly worth the effort in laying out the bin to reduce the hours of labor.

This is the easiest way we have found to make compost with a minimum of labor. The saving on the lesser amount of manure required repays us for the work of running the compost through the shredder. Actually, the cost of the compost is about equal to the cost of manure, and we have a much better product.

We have used such compost on other plants besides the vegetable garden, like roses, clematis, and dwarf fruit trees. In every case, its use has produced extraordinary results.

After the first heavy frost, the shredded compost is spread over the garden as evenly as possible, about half an inch deep. The soil is then in top condition to work. It is infinitely easier to do this work in October than in the spring, when the soil is wet and everything is in a rush. Then a garden tractor or rototiller is used to incorporate the compost with the garden soil. The machine mixes the soil and compost very thoroughly and does a first-rate job.

Whether to make and use garden compost is something that each gardener has to work out for himself; it is very difficult to lay down hard-and-fast rules. Farm manure, space for the compost piles, and the labor to build them all must be available.

This procedure may sound complicated to the less serious

gardener, and a compost pile can be maintained on a smaller scale. A shredder is not essential, although obviously it is an advantage. But do not oversimplify to the point of trying to get by with only one compost bin. The compost that is ready for use will get buried so deeply that it will be almost impossible for you to get at it. It is best to have one bin with compost ready to use and one bin to use when you clean up the garden and yard.

Fertilizers

All plants require certain elements for satisfactory growth. Some of these are obtained from air and water and most come from the soil. The elements that plants need the most are, unfortunately, the ones usually lacking: nitrogen, phosphorous, potassium, and calcium. The common commercial fertilizers consist of nitrogen (N), phosphorus (P), and potassium (K) in various proportions. The only way to determine which proportions your garden needs is by having a soil test. Never guess what elements are lacking in your soil. Various state and county agencies provide soil testing services, and you can buy your own soil testing kit. Contact your county agricultural extension office or agricultural colleges for information. The soil test will determine which nutrients are lacking so that you will know which type of fertilizer you need.

The soil test will also determine the acidity or alkalinity of your garden. This is measured on the pH scale, ranging from 0 (acid) to 14 (alkaline); 7.0 is neutral. The best range for most plants is 6.0–6.8. Again, it is unwise to guess and take for granted that your soil needs ground limestone, although that is often the case, especially in New England. An excess of either acidity or alkalinity will be detrimental. Beets are a good indicator of an excess in either direction; the roots will be stunted and there will be too much yellow and red in the leaves.

The fertilizers are broadcast uniformly over the garden in the early spring, then worked into the soil with the first plowing. A rainy day is ideal for this procedure. Be very careful when using commercial fertilizer and also fresh manure after your garden is planted. Side dressing is risky business; tender, young seedlings are easily damaged by fertilizer or fresh manure burn.

In addition to compost, we use 5–10–10 fertilizer (representing percentages of nitrogen, phosphorus, and potassium) on all vegetables (except asparagus) at the rate of fifty pounds per 1000 square feet, and superphosphate at the rate of eight pounds per 1000 square feet. Both are broadcast over the garden in early spring. 0–20–20 is broadcast over the asparagus bed about April 15 at the rate of forty pounds per 1000 square feet.

TOOLS

A well-stocked tool shed is a necessity if you intend to take up vegetable gardening. Certain tools are best suited to only one specific and rather limited function, but others are useful for a number of jobs. Yet the list of absolute necessities is short and should require only a reasonable outlay. There are probably as many gadgets advertised in magazines and seed catalogs as there are gardeners, and a large number seem about as useful to us as a one-pronged spade fork. Each gardener soon develops personal preferences, and one man's superweeder may be another's dust collector in the tool shed. After several annoying experiences, we decided to adhere to one rule: stick to quality. Nothing is more irritating than breaking a poorly made hoe in the midst of planting on a Sunday when the stores are closed. But even the best implements occasionally fall apart, so it is handy to have a spare of frequently used tools in reserve.

The following is a list of those tools that we consider the minimum necessary for a small garden: wheelbarrow; long-handled, round-pointed shovel; long-handled and short-handled cultivators; D-handle spade fork; pointed trowel; hand pruning shears; asparagus knife; hose and sprinkler; watering can; onion hoe (long — 7 inch narrow blade); standard planter hoe (5 inch blade); scuffle hoe; steel-bow rake with rigid teeth; lawn rake; and 3½-gallon sprayer. As time passes, you may find other tools worth the investment:

mechanical seeder, compost shredder, electric clippers, fertilizer spreader, and perhaps more. With proper care, all of your tools should last many years, and their lives can be extended by a thorough washing and oiling before winter storage. Also, shears, edgers, and hoes should be sharpened frequently.

Rototillers can be rented on a daily basis, but the investment in a small, two-wheel garden tractor is almost essential. Ours is a Gravely, which we highly recommend as one of the few products on the market today that live up to their advertisements. A number of attachments are available, four of which save hours of back-breaking labor in the garden. The field plow is used to turn the soil initially in the spring, and can also be used for grinding up a field into some semblance of a garden. The cultivator attachment, which pulverizes the soil at a shallower depth, is used throughout the summer to weed between rows and prepare seed beds. Use of the latter requires a garden of sufficient size to permit a space of at least 3 feet between rows. We also have a 30-inch

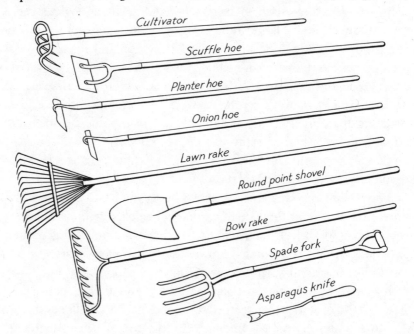

Cultivator

Scuffle hoe

Planter hoe

Onion hoe

Lawn rake

Round point shovel

Bow rake

Spade fork

Asparagus knife

rotary mower to clean up dead vegetation, such as corn stalks and tomato vines in the fall. After the mowing has been done, the debris can be raked up and composted. Finally, the 20-gallon sprayer can cut hours off the time it takes to spray insecticides and fungicides with a smaller unit.

Storing tools and equipment in a work shed is the best way to keep them orderly and to provide you with work space. A solid bench for potting, with bins for vermiculite, peat moss, garden loam, leaf mold, sand, and so on underneath is quite useful. You may want to include a small locker, lined with galvanized iron, which is mouse-proof, for the storage of seeds. Shelves can be added for flats, pots, and crockery, and pegboard on the walls is an excellent way to keep small, and easy to lose, hand tools. A separate area can be set aside for storing wire fencing, iron stakes, pipe, and other miscellaneous gear. While it may seem something of an extravagance, both electricity for light and power tools and running water should be included.

The Skinner sprinkler system is quite effective. This system is simply pipes with nozzles, spaced about 3 feet apart, running the full width of the garden; the pipes are spaced about 50 feet apart. The pipes can be rotated by hand so that the line of jets can face any desired position. With water at fifty-pounds' pressure, the sprinklers will squirt water on either side of the pipe as desired up to 25 feet from the pipe. If the water pressure is less than fifty pounds, the pipes should be closer together. If the wind is blowing, they will not sprinkle so far. Sprinklers that work mechanically are available, but for vegetable garden purposes, it is better to set the pipes by hand, pointing them to the desired area and letting them run. In this way, water is not wasted on areas that don't need it.

Part Two

In writing a section on each vegetable, it seemed advisable to make the sections as uniform as possible. At the beginning of each section is a résumé showing the varieties grown, the dates of planting and maturing, and the amount planted. The dates given are those used at Candlewood. We plant our first peas, corn, and beans at about the same dates that are generally used in this locality. For other localities, the same method can be followed and the later plantings adjusted in accordance with the first plantings. If a record is kept of the planting and maturing dates for one year, it is very easy to change the planting dates for the following year. Next follows the various varieties we have tried and some information about them. The difficulties, if any, are then discussed. After that, our procedure of growing is described. If the vegetable is used in the winter, the method of storing is described. Remarks on cooking complete most sections.

This method leads to repetition in various sections, but, since this book is not a novel, it seems more important to give full and complete *information about each vegetable, rather than ask the reader to turn to several chapters to get the complete story.*

The data given were obtained by personal experience only in this garden. Some of the yields of the vegetables are high, but there is no doubt that many people obtain still higher yields on certain vegetables in particularly favored spots. At any rate, it is interesting to have figures that can be used for comparison.

The varieties chosen are the results of over 700 seed tests. Just to make these tests would require a garden 20 feet wide and 1400 feet long, with the rows planted at an average of 2 feet apart!

Asparagus

Candlewood vegetable rating	100
Variety: Waltham Washington	*Source:* Seedway
Number of rows	10
Rows planted	3 ft. apart
In the row plants	18 in. apart
Size of plot	30 × 76 ft. = 2280 sq. ft.
Season	May 1–June 22
For winter use	Freeze — Results excellent

ASPARAGUS that has been properly grown, picked, and cooked is the best of all vegetables. Its season with us in Ipswich is from May 1 to June 22. During that period, we have asparagus every day and love it.

In Ipswich, the first asparagus is ready to cut about April 28, never earlier than April 15 or later than May 9. This is a big spread in the dates — more so than for any other vegetable. Since these dates are for the first pickings, they are not to be relied on completely as an indication of when the season actually starts. Over the years, we have noticed that, frequently, the second picking of asparagus may not be picked within six days, but that the third picking generally is close after the second. To save yourself disappointment, it is better to consider that the asparagus season officially starts with the second picking, which is usually May 1. There is little difference among varieties in the start of the harvest; it depends on the spring weather.

Unless you live in California, the chances are fairly good that

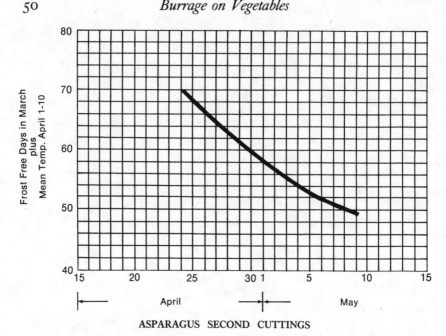

ASPARAGUS SECOND CUTTINGS

The easy and interesting way of predicting when asparagus will be ready for
continuous cutting. Simply note the last date in March when the ground was
free of frost, count the number of frost-free days, and add to it the average
temperature of the first ten days in April. Look on the curve and read on the
lowest line when the second cutting of asparagus will be available.

you are not going to be able to buy good fresh asparagus.
Asparagus two days old or older just can't compare with what
comes fresh from your garden. One of the tricks of the market
gardener is to let the stalks grow about 1 foot long before cutting
it. This may fool the housewife into buying a lot of asparagus, but
the quality is definitely lowered.

VARIETIES

We have tried and tested asparagus seeds from six countries. If
you intend to start a new bed, we recommend Waltham Washington, which is more rust-resistant than the old standby, Mary
Washington. The former was developed by Professor Young at
the Waltham Field Station and produces consistently greater yields.

YIELDS

We like asparagus so much that we should like to have it every day during the season and also freeze enough to have it twice a week during the winter.

To determine how many plants you need, all you have to do is estimate how many stalks you would like to have for each person, and multiply that by the number of people and by the times you would like to have asparagus during the season. Then add the quantity you would like to freeze. If you are fond of asparagus, you will soon have astronomical figures. At Candlewood, we have twice increased the size of the bed and could use still more. But, for practical purposes, if you had asparagus every other day of the fifty-day season, that would mean 25 times at 15 stalks per person which would make 375 stalks, or about 40 plants per person. If you want some to freeze, you should plant more.

DIFFICULTIES

We have had our bed for many years and, to date, we have experienced only two difficulties. First, we had some asparagus beetles, but they were so few and did so little damage that we hardly classify them as a difficulty. We did have a certain procedure for handling them; the small stalks, which were too small to eat, were allowed to grow as they appeared. By the end of the season there were about 100 small stalks in the bed. What beetles there were collected on these stalks; as soon as the cutting was over, we sprayed with a mixture of DDT and Pyrox, which is now forbidden. Modern day asparagus beetles are easily dispatched by the spraying of any one of the following: Sevin (a brand name), rotenone, or malathion.

Our other difficulty is more serious; at the end of fifteen years about 55 roots of the original asparagus plants died. This is 11 percent of the 500 plants. One-year roots should be planted annually to replace those that die.

PROCEDURE

An asparagus bed should last fifteen to twenty years. Once established, the cost and labor of maintaining it are so low, and the yield from it so high, that the cost of making the finest possible bed is certainly justified. It seems to us that there is no vegetable or fruit in the garden that gives as much pleasure as a good asparagus bed. By all means, plant the best you can. Prepare it with the greatest of care, for, once planted and until you start a new one (perhaps twenty years later), you can do very little to help your plants. Of all places to use manure in large quantities, an asparagus bed is the one that is most justified.

The case history of the Candlewood bed of 500 plants in 10 rows, 76 feet long, runs as follows. (For a smaller bed, the figures can be scaled down proportionately.)

In February, 3200 seedlings were started from about two ounces of seed in two flats.

In April, when the seedlings were 2 or 3 inches high and starting to feather, 1600 of the straightest and sturdiest were chosen for the first transplanting. These were transplanted into flats and carried along in the coldframes until the last of June. This required forty-six flats, 17 x 10½ x 3 inches, which take up a lot of room. If you don't wish to bother, or have no coldframe, then persuade your local nurseryman to do the job for you.

In June, 1200 were again selected as in April. These were planted 1½ inches deep in a temporary bed, 10 rows, 1½ feet apart; the plants were set 8 inches apart, or 113 in a row. The bed, 16½ x 76 feet (1254 square feet), was prepared by spading in well-rotted horse manure and was top-dressed with a garden fertilizer, 5–10–10, at the rate of forty pounds to 1000 square feet, or fifty pounds for the bed.

After frost, the plants were mulched with straw for the winter.

In November, the new permanent bed, measuring 30 x 76 feet, was prepared by trenching, as follows:

A trench was opened up two spades deep (about 18 inches) and the soil carried to the other end of the bed. Another trench was dug alongside the first. The topsoil from the second trench was put on the bottom of the first, and a good dressing, about 4 inches deep, of manure was spread over it and forked in. The subsoil of the second trench was then placed on top in the first trench. The entire bed was done in this manner; the second trench was filled in with the soil taken from the first one.

On the first of April of the following year, ten trenches were dug in the bed described, each 12 inches deep, 15 inches wide, and 3 feet apart, center to center. Three inches of manure were spread in the trenches and forked in. Four pounds of garden fertilizer, 5–10–10, were added to each trench, or forty pounds for the entire bed. The soil was tested and the necessary amount of ground limestone was added. (Soil should test at pH 6.5 or higher.) This seems like a tough job — and it was. Back-breaking and expensive, to say the least, but when it was done, look what we had — a bed 18 inches deep filled with manure, fertilizers, and limestone that will last for years.

On April 15, 500 of the best plants were chosen for the final beds. Only enough plants were dug at one time to fill one trench, and they were protected against drying out. The roots were planted about 18 inches apart and about 6 inches below the level of the garden; then they were covered with 3 inches of soil so that the finished trench was 3 inches below the level of the garden. As soon as the spears started coming through the ground, soil was thrown in, a little at a time; this was continued until the bed was level with the garden. Two years after we started the seed, we cut a few stalks; the third year we had a good crop, which we cut for only one month. This gave the plants a good chance to grow, and the following year they produced a full crop. Ordinarily we stop cutting asparagus about June 21, which is about the time the first peas grown in the garden are picked.

About Apr. 15	An 0–20–20 fertilizer is broadcast over the bed at the rate of 40 lbs. per 1000 sq. ft. and worked in with a 3-pronged cultivator. Then the bed is smoothed over with a wooden rake. During the cutting season the bed is weeded as necessary.
About June 20	The bed is weeded thoroughly to rid it of the broad leaf, perennial weeds, such as dandelions and plantain. The safest way to do this is by hand, with a weeding tool. Simazine or diuron can be used for annual weeds.
About Nov. 1	The asparagus canes are cut down. The organic garden compost is then spread over the bed ½ in. deep, which is at the rate of ⅓ cord per 1000 sq. ft., or 14 cords per acre.
About Nov. 15	Farm manure is spread over the bed 1½ in. deep, which is at the rate of 1 cord per 1000 sq. ft., or 43 cords per acre.

By fall the plants will grow to an average height of at least 5 feet, and some will grow 7 feet high with stems 1½ inches in diameter. The bed is so thick that it is impossible to walk through it, and it looks like a small forest. In the late summer or early fall, after a rain or heavy dew, there is nothing more lovely to look at than a thick growth of asparagus plants with the sun shining on the drops of moisture. They look like acres of diamonds glistening in the sun.

In November, the bed is cut close after the plants have dried. Every two years enough ground limestone is applied to bring the soil to pH 6.5. Asparagus needs plenty of water. Have a sprinkler system for your bed if possible.

The taller the stalk grows above ground, the more bitter and tough it becomes. The market gardener often lets the stalks grow more than a foot long. It is true that this practice produces large green stalks with sales appeal, and premium prices are obtained, but actually the quality is not as good as when the stalks are cut before they are more than 5 inches above the soil. Stalks, so cut, are whiter, more tender, and have much better flavor and texture. They may not have the maximum amounts of vitamins, but they do have the quality. Try cutting at different heights to see which you prefer.

WINTER USE

Asparagus is well suited for freezing. Of all the vegetables to put in a freezer, this is one of the best. It maintains its quality, at least, until April. It is easy to prepare and freeze.

One standard bunch will fill a pint package. There are approximately 27 stalks, ½ inch in diameter, to a standard bunch. We find that 1 pint package is enough for two people, but one person can easily consume a pint package without any trouble. For two people we put up 80 pint boxes, or 3 per week for the 6 fall and winter months. Plastic bags may also be used for packaging the bunches.

COOKING

The skins of the stalks are bitter, so be sure to peel them. With a knife, this is a difficult job, and it takes about 30 minutes to peel 60 stalks of ¾ inch size. With an asparagus peeler, the job can be done easily in 12 minutes. By all means use the peeler gadget; it saves time and does a better job. Cut the asparagus to the desired length. Then peel down the stalk, resting the root end of the stalk on the table, and wash. The peeled stalks are bright and clean looking, and their appearance is greatly improved.

Use the Mystery Chef Method, as follows:
  Wash the asparagus.
  Boil rapidly 2 quarts of water in a 3-quart enamel pot.
  Add 1 teaspoon of baking soda and then the asparagus.
  Cook for 2 minutes after water returns to boil; it is
    important to leave the asparagus uncovered.
  If the water foams, skim off the foam and reduce the heat.
  Strain off water and return asparagus to pot.
  Have water boiling rapidly in another 3-quart pot, metal
    or enamel.
  Add 3 tablespoons of salt to boiling water.
  Add this boiling salt water to the asparagus in the enamel
    pot.
  Cook for 8 minutes uncovered.
  Strain the asparagus and return to pot.
  Add butter and salt.

To cook frozen asparagus, take it directly from the freezer and
place it in hot water for 5 minutes. This will thaw it and bring it to
room temperature for cooking.

Meanwhile, buttered toast and melted butter, to which has been
added a little lemon juice, should be made ready. Sprinkle over
each piece of buttered toast about ½ teaspoon of the water in which
the asparagus has been cooked. Place the asparagus on the toast
and pour the melted butter over it.

For years, most cooking experts have been violently opposed to
the use of baking soda, but this method uses soda for only 2
minutes, and we are convinced that no harm is done. Even if some
of the vitamins are destroyed, we would still advocate this method
because asparagus, home-raised and cooked by this method, is
something from the clouds. No better food exists. The best
asparagus bought in the market and cooked in this fashion is only
about 75 percent as good. The delay between cutting and cooking,
the fact that market asparagus is not cut until it is high above the
ground, and, finally, the poor kind of asparagus grown all are
factors that impair the quality. The same asparagus cooked in the

manner generally used (slightly scraped and then boiled for 20 minutes), is only about 25 percent as good and is simply not worth eating.

Pressure Cooking Method

If you do not want to use soda, then the pressure cooker is the next best bet. This will produce asparagus about 85 percent as good as the first method. Some cooks are afraid of the pressure cooker, but it is very easy to use if you give it a little thought and a little care.

Put ¼ cup of water in the cooker, add the peeled asparagus, put the cover on the cooker, and place the cooker on the stove with the vent pipe open. Since air in the cooker will interfere with the cooking, all the air must be driven out. This is done by heating the pot and leaving the vent open until a small stream of steam comes out of the vent pipe. Then place the pressure valve over the vent pipe and cook at 15 pounds of pressure for 2 minutes.

Then, without disturbing the pressure valve, place the cooker under running cold water and cool all over; this takes ½ minute. The steam will condense and the pressure be reduced to normal. The valve can then be removed without danger and the cover taken off.

Asparagus should be served on toast with plenty of butter, on very hot plates, all by itself. Of all the vegetables, none is more worthy to be served as a special course.

Beans

Candlewood vegetable rating   95

Varieties: Topcrop	*Source:* Burpee
Tendercrop	*Source:* Harris

Seed treatment	Captan
Number of plantings	12
Seed required for 75 ft. of row	½ lb.
Depth of planting	1–1½ in.
Distance between rows	2–3 ft.
Distance between seeds	2–3 in.
Pest control for Mexican bean beetle	Diazinon, Sevin, rotenone, or malathion
Average number of days required to reach maturity	52
Season: Garden	July 4–October 10
Coldframe	October 4–October 30
For winter use	Freeze

PLANTING SCHEDULE IN IPSWICH

Plant	Begin	Finish	Days to maturity	Quality (%)
Apr. 15	July 1	July 10	77	85
May 12	July 7	July 18	56	100
May 30	July 18	July 29	49	100
June 14	July 29	Aug. 9	45	100
June 25	Aug. 9	Aug. 20	45	100
July 5	Aug. 20	Aug. 31	46	100
July 14	Aug. 31	Sept. 11	48	90
July 24	Sept. 11	Sept. 22	49	90
Aug. 1	Sept. 22	Oct. 3	52	90
Aug. 6	Sept. 30	Oct. 10	55	90
(frame) Aug. 8	Oct. 10	Oct. 18	68	90
(frame) Aug. 14	Oct. 20	Oct. 30	73	85

*

VARIETIES

We have tried the following with good results.

Variety	Quality	Variety	Quality
Topcrop	Excellent	Keystonian	Good
Asgrow Black Valentine	Excellent	Logan	Good
		Metis	Good
Longreen	Excellent	New Long Tendergreen	Good
Supergreen	Excellent	Noir Hatif de Belgique	Good
Tenderpod	Excellent	Plentiful	Good
Wade	Excellent	Prince	Good
Tendercrop	Excellent	Rival	Good
Du Perreux	Good	Stringless Greenpod	Good
Empereur	Good		

Others tried:

Bountiful	Conserva
Burpee's Stringless	Prizewinner
Commodore Green Pod Imperial	Tendergreen

Pole beans tried:

Horticultural	New Italian
Homestead Stringless	Pole, Italian
Kentucky Wonder	Scotia

Of all vegetables, green snap beans are the most satisfactory to grow in the home garden. They can be grown over a long season, and even the novice can produce a crop of superb quality. Furthermore, in addition to being easy to grow, they are relatively free from disease, produce a high yield considering the amount of space needed, and during the growing season they are attractive to look at. What more could one want?

Some people say they do not like beans; when you begin to ask questions, you find that they have never had their own garden.

How could they ever know what a delicacy good beans really are? The ordinary restaurant serves beans of such low quality that you might as well eat hay.

Beans love warm weather and will not germinate fully in cold soil. If they are planted before April 21, they will not, on the average, mature any earlier than those planted on April 21. However, we plant on April 15 just in case there is a very early spring. If beans are planted after August 10, they will not mature at all. Beans are one of the only two vegetables — carrots are the other — that are grown during the whole season from only one variety. For many vegetables, two or more varieties are used in order to obtain the best quality possible during the different parts of the season. According to our experience, beans of the highest quality can be picked from a row for about eleven days. If the row is only partially picked, we have found that after about twelve days the pods become large and tough. The rows, therefore, are planted so that they will mature just eleven days apart, except that the second row is planted so that it will mature six days after the first row.

When the first row matures, it is somewhat of an occasion; consequently, we are likely to use beans in rather large quantities. To obtain maturing dates eleven days apart, plant the third row eighteen days after the second row; each succeeding row is planted after fewer days, until the last row is planted only five days after the preceding one. Of course, if there are several days of unseasonable heat or cold, the maturing dates are slightly upset, but not as much as you might expect. One advantage of planting only one variety is that the maturing dates of the whole patch of beans are moved either forward or backward as a group. If several varieties are planted, the extra heat or cold will affect different varieties in dissimilar ways so that it is almost impossible to count on having the beans mature at intervals exactly eleven days apart without making unnecessary plantings.

We have tried many varieties through the years, although we have had little incentive to experiment since we discovered a good variety in the very beginning. Topcrop has a lot to recommend it. It is early; the pod is straight and plump; the yield is good; and it is easy to pick and easy to handle in the kitchen. When it is cooked, it lies flat on the plate and, because of its bright green color, is most attractive to look at. Eye appeal, you know, plays its part in the enjoyment of quality vegetables. Tendercrop has been equally successful at Craigston garden and it is particularly recommended if you intend to do much freezing. The yield is the highest of any vegetable at Craigston, and beans from the freezer are the mainstay of the winter vegetable diet. One word of caution is in order here: one should avoid selecting any variety on the sole basis of its suitability for freezing. You may well end up with a mediocre fare during the summer and beans of acceptable or better quality during the winter. It is much akin to buying a new coat one size too large for your child, hoping that it will last two seasons. What often happens is that it turns out to be too large the first year and too small the second. Get the proper size coat and the best variety of beans. If you must, select two varieties — one that is best suited for freezing and one that is best for summer consumption.

Pole beans undoubtedly produce greater pounds per square foot of area than bush beans, but aside from that we can see no reason for growing them. The quality of those that we have tried is not as good as that of bush beans; the bean beetle attacks their foliage quite badly so that it looks unattractive; the poles are a bother to put up; it seems harder to obtain a steady continuity of fresh young beans. The most important drawback to their use is that pole beans do not mature until twelve to fifteen days after the bush beans mature. Certainly there isn't much point in missing two weeks during which you might be eating bush beans. You will have to make your own decision and the best way to decide is to try both kinds.

If you do choose to try pole beans as a space saver, be sure to remember that they should be planted on the north side of your garden. They will not shade the neighboring crop and will provide some wind protection. Rough, straight poles, 10 feet long, should be freshly cut each year. We have found either chokecherry or maple to be ideal for this purpose. The poles should be planted 2 feet in the ground to prevent their being blown over in a high wind. You will be digging into the subsoil unless your topsoil is quite thick; be sure to replace the subsoil in the hole first so that it does not come into contact with the surface roots of the bean plants. If the poles are any longer than 10 feet, you will need a stepladder to harvest the beans! Five to six seeds should be planted at a distance of about 4 inches from the base of the pole and at a depth of about 2 inches. When the first set of leaves has developed, the plants should be thinned so that the three strongest remain.

We grew, for two years, Italian pole beans. As snap beans, their quality was only fair, but they are good for soup. For soup use, they should not be picked until the seeds in the pods are fully matured. They can be stored and used all winter. Inasmuch as these dried beans can be easily procured in winter, it did not seem sensible to grow them even though the soup was good.

We have tried only two varieties of yellow bush or wax beans; both were decidedly secondary to the palate to green beans and we have therefore eliminated them from our garden. A good guide to their desirability, in our opinion, is the relative space they occupy in various seed catalogs. Certainly this is not the only measure, but it does seem a good indication to the beginner for establishing priorities.

PROCEDURE

In the late fall, at Candlewood, compost is spread over the garden, about ½ inch thick; we can use more if it is available. This is a voluminous amount and more than most gardeners have at their disposal. Ground limestone is also applied when necessary, about once every two years. The compost and the limestone are then spaded in, or preferably worked in with a rototiller, which does an excellent job of thoroughly mixing the compost with the soil. The next spring we spread fertilizer over the garden and work it in.

If you use bean seeds from Harris, they will be pretreated with captan, a mild fungicide that improves germination. If your seeds are not treated, we think it is worth your treating them.

The Mexican bean beetle, the most common pest that attacks beans, can be kept under control by dusting or spraying with any one of the following: Diazinon, Sevin, rotenone, or malathion. If you use the standard cylinder-type sprayer, be sure to direct the spray on the underside of the leaves as well as the top and the stems. The wire fence recommended earlier will keep the local rabbit population from enjoying its favorite feast.

We have found the use of a thick mulch, about 4 inches deep, of salt-marsh straw or salt-marsh hay, is very effective. It improves both the quality of the beans and, eventually, the quality of the soil, increases the yield, and completely eliminates the necessity for weeding.

By using a permanent coldframe with high sides, we are able to extend the season until the end of October.

WINTER USE

At Craigston, we freeze more beans than any other vegetable. We prepare them in a variety of ways: cut up in $\frac{1}{4}$ inch sections, whole, or sliced lengthwise with a gadget made especially for the purpose. We can find only a negligible difference in quality between frozen beans consumed in November and those consumed in April. The deterioration process is slowed considerably by keeping the freezer at as low a setting as possible, so we freeze enough to last all winter. For a family of four, this amounts to about 55 pint cartons of cut beans and 25 meal-sized bags of whole or sliced beans. If the beans are grown properly and frozen properly, the average home gardener should be able to produce a winter fare significantly superior to the commercially available counterpart. Try it and you will never go back to Mr. Birdseye!

COOKING

Beans are an outstandingly good vegetable if the right variety is chosen, if they are picked at the right time, and if they are properly cooked.

There is some part of a bean's composition that, when cooked, gives the bean the characteristics of rubber. If a bean is sliced lengthwise into long, thin strips and then cooked, this unpleasant component is either washed out or destroyed by the cooking. In any event, the beans that have been sliced lengthwise certainly taste different from others and their quality is definitely improved. The slicing of beans seems to act in the same way as the peeling of asparagus. It takes only a few moments and is worth doing. Beans look more attractive at the table if they are tied up in little bundles before they are cooked. The strings, of course, should be removed before the beans are served.

Use the Mystery Chef Method, as follows:
Wash the beans.
Boil rapidly 2 quarts of water in a 3-quart enamel pot.
Add 1 teaspoon of baking soda and then the beans.
Cook for 1 minute uncovered; it is important to leave the beans uncovered. If water foams, skim off the foam and reduce the heat.
Strain off water and return the beans to pot.
Have water boiling rapidly in another 3-quart enamel or metal pot.
Add 3 tablespoons of salt to the boiling water.
Add this boiling salt water to the beans in the enamel pot.
Cook uncovered young beans 5 minutes, longer for old.
Strain the beans and return to pot.
Add butter and salt.

Beans are at their best when served on toast with butter on very hot plates, as a separate course. If you really want to do a job, soften the toast with a little of the water in which the beans are cooked. Topcrop beans prepared this way are so much better than ordinary beans, that there is just no comparison. No one will leave a single bean on the plate.

SUMMARY

1. *Use Topcrop variety.*
2. *Wet the trench in which the seeds are planted.*
3. *Make many plantings.*
4. *Spray to control Mexican bean beetle.*
5. *Cook by Mystery Chef Method.*
6. *Serve as a separate course.*

Beets

Candlewood vegetable rating   80

Varieties: Ruby Queen   Source: Harris
          Red Ball (late)   Source: Burpee

Seed treatment   Captan or red oxide of copper
Size of plots: Hotframe   4½ × 6 ft.
        Garden   8 × 38 ft. = 304 sq. ft.
Rows planted   1 ft. apart
Number of rows (excluding
        hotframe)   8
Seed required for 100 ft. of row   1 oz.
Seed required for this bed
    with 304 ft. of row:
        Ruby Queen   2 oz.
        Red Ball   2 oz.
Season: Young beets,
        hotframe   May 24–June 10
Young beets, garden   June 18–Dec. 1
Mature beets   Use only for soup

PLANTING SCHEDULE IN IPSWICH

Start green-house	Plant	Variety	Location	Begin	Finish	Quality (%)
Feb. 20	Apr. 1	Ruby Queen*	Hotframe	May 24	June 10	75
	Apr. 15	Ruby Queen	Garden	June 18	Aug. 1	100
	May 1	Ruby Queen	Garden	June 28	Aug. 1	100
	May 1	Ruby Queen	Garden	June 28	Aug. 1	100
	May 1	Ruby Queen	Garden	June 28	Aug. 1	100
	May 9	Ruby Queen	Garden	July 7	Sept. 1	100
	June 7	Red Ball	Garden	Aug. 1	Dec. 1	100
	June 27	Red Ball	Garden	Aug. 23	Dec. 1	100
	July 9	Red Ball	Garden	Sept. 15	Dec. 1	90

* Transplant.
The May 1 rows are used for processing.

Beets are generally considered an uninteresting vegetable, and that is a correct evaluation of the beets sold in the market. In fact, most beets can be classed simply as food; you eat them only as a last resort. But young beets are quite different. Picked early when they are small in size, up to $1\frac{1}{4}$ inches in diameter, they are really delicious to eat — tender and sweet. There is just as much difference between new and mature beets as there is between new and mature potatoes. Until we found the Red Ball variety, it never seemed to us that beets were worth eating after September 15. Although their quality begins to fall off slightly, they are still good to eat up to the time the ground freezes solid.

Any large beets that may be left in the rows are used for making beet soup. They are better for that purpose than young ones.

VARIETIES

We have tried a number of different varieties, and we have also compared seeds of a single variety bought from several sources. Harvard, in our opinion, used to be the best tasting, had the best texture, and was the variety we selected for the earliest plantings. But Harvard is no longer available, and we think Ruby Queen an excellent substitute. For the late plantings, we use Red Ball. This is the only late-planted variety grown at Candlewood, that is worth eating.

We have tried the following with good results.

Variety	Quality
Ruby Queen	Excellent
Red Ball	Excellent
Crosby Egyptian	Good

Others tried:

Detroit Dark Red	Harvard
Early Blood Turnip	Long Season
Beats All	

DIFFICULTIES

In the past, cutworms have given a little trouble, but can now be destroyed by using Diazinon.

The only real trouble we had in growing beets was that we used to find a part of each row and, occasionally, nearly a whole row in which either the beet seeds did not germinate at all or, if they did, the plants died from damping-off when they were about 1 inch tall.

We made, in addition to our regular plantings, many experimental plantings to obtain the answers to the following questions:

1. How could we obtain satisfactory germination?
2. How could we prevent damping-off?

The conclusions of our experiments are as follows:

1. Germination

We believe poor germination is due to one or more of these conditions.

Planting too early. We have found at Candlewood that planting before April 1 was a complete failure. Practically none of the seeds survived, no matter what variety we used or what treatment we gave them. Of the seeds planted between April 1 and April 10, about one-half survived. Seeds planted April 15 or later gave completely satisfactory results if they were treated as described later. Probably every garden has its own critical dates and these must be determined The seeds that did survive April 1 planting, bore on June 10. This is only five days earlier than the seeds planted on April 15. As a result of these experiments, we settled on April 15 for the earliest planting date in the garden.

Too much manure. Our garden is divided into two halves; what is grown one year on one half is grown on the other the next year. We found that we obtained an immediate improvement in germination if we did not use manure in the area in which the beets were to be planted. This area did receive manure the following year when other crops were planted there. For the last few years, however, we have been using garden compost each year. We also learned that using compost every year is better than using manure every other year.

Not enough lime. Our soil tested pH 6.1. We added enough ground limestone to bring the soil to pH 6.5, tried again, and found there was an improvement.

2. *Damping-off*

The term damping-off is applied to the decay of young seedlings at or near the surface of the ground caused by the action of organisms. When some of the little plants were about 1 inch tall, and would suddenly die, we found it a most unhappy experience. You can't then replant and have the row mature at the desired time; it is too late. It simply means that you won't have beets when you want them. We tried a number of remedies and used to coat the seeds with red oxide of copper. This worked exceedingly well except when the ground was wet, in which case we pregerminated the seeds and then coated them with the red oxide. Some beet seeds available today will be pretreated with captan.

PROCEDURE

From the planting schedule, it can be seen that very early beets can be obtained by the use of a hotframe. We found that it was better to start the seeds in the greenhouse and then transplant to the hotframe rather than to plant directly in the hotframe. Beets from transplanted plants are about five days earlier and are of better quality than those planted directly in the frame.

We have tried to grow beets in the coldframes that we use for corn and peas, but have never been successful, although we have successfully grown lettuce this way. Sometimes a few beets will grow, but, generally, the yield is very poor. This might be due to the fact that they are shaded by the peas and corn.

As a result of many experiments, we now use the following procedure, which works satisfactorily:

1. In the plot where the beets are to be planted, we use compost each year.

2. To prevent damage from cutworms, the ground is sprayed with Diazinon.

3. In the early fall, the plot to be planted is tested for acidity, and enough ground limestone is added to bring the soil to pH 6.5.

4. We make a small trench in which the seeds are to be planted, and sprinkle the trench well with 5–10–10.

5. Because the soil of the garden at Candlewood is quite wet at the first planting, April 15, and sometimes the second, the seedlings damp-off. We have found that pregerminating the seeds and coating them with red copper oxide completely overcomes this trouble. It is somewhat of a nuisance to do, but, if we want early beets, it is the only way we can have them. At that, it is a lot better to make the effort and have the beets, rather than simply to plant the beet seeds and then discover that most of the seedlings are killed. We have used the following procedure for pregermination.

a. Obtain a sieve with a mesh screen that is just fine enough to prevent the beet seeds from passing through. An 18-mesh screen is satisfactory for the variety we use. Obtain some very fine sand and screen enough of it to fill a glass.

b. Soak the beet seeds in warm water for 8 hours.

c. Strain the seeds.

d. Mix the seed with the screened sand and let stand for ½ hour. The dry sand will absorb the water remaining on the seeds.

e. Put the mixture of seeds and sand in the sieve. The sand will pass through and leave the dry seeds in the sieve. Wet seeds are very difficult to sow and this is an easy way to obviate the difficulty.

f. Coat the seeds with red copper oxide by putting a teaspoon of the copper in a pint jar, adding the seeds, and shaking the jar.

This method has worked well for us for many years, and it has absolutely prevented the bare patches in the early rows that we used to have. As soon as the ground is dry, the pregerminating of the seed is not necessary; dusting the seeds with the red copper oxide is sufficient.

6. Because beet seeds are relatively small, they are difficult to sow. Either too few or, what is more common, too many seeds are planted, so that thinning the rows later becomes a very tedious task. It is worthwhile to use a mechanical seed sower, which will greatly reduce the labor of thinning.

Plant the seeds; cover them with loam; firm down and sprinkle with water if dry. This method makes all the seeds germinate, and there is a little quick fertilizer to give them a good start.

The rows are thinned so that the beets are about 2 inches apart. In this way they grow quickly, are not misshapen from crowding, and all those in a row mature at about the same time. Since there are not many in a row, those of one planting are generally eaten before the next planting matures.

7. We use salt-marsh straw or hay as a mulch on the beet bed, as we do for carrots. The waving heads of bronze beet tops interspersed with the rows of slender carrot tops make one of the prettiest pictures in the garden. It is so lovely it seems a shame to pick the vegetables. The mulch is certainly worth using, for hardly a weed is seen and the quality of the beets is improved. The use of mulch in the beet bed pays greater dividends than anywhere else in the garden.

Beet Greens

It is generally recommended that the beet rows be thinned and the beet greens that are picked be eaten. To us this sounds like the reasoning of a New England conscience. Thin, but don't bother with beet greens. They won't taste any better just because they are thinnings. If you doubt this, cook some spinach and beet greens under identical conditions and see which is the better.

YIELDS

In a way, it seems foolish to talk about yields when you deliberately plan to pick the beets at the point at which they are one-quarter to one-half grown. But if you want the best beets you ever tasted, that is the time to eat them. The 8 rows planted give us all the beets we need; of these 8 rows, there are 2 rows set aside for processing. The 2 rows give us 30 pint bottles of beets, which are enough to supply us with beets for the winter. After Christmas, the quality falls off slightly, but they are still pleasant to eat in April.

WINTER USE

Storing. It is my belief that stored beets are not good to eat. They just get poorer and poorer and become an affront to the eye.

Freezing. Better than storing, but beets do not freeze as well as other vegetables, such as peas.

COOKING

Select beets 1 to 1¼ inches in diameter, wash, and, without cutting up, boil until a fork can be stuck into the beets — about 15 minutes. If the beets are bigger, more time will be required.

When the beets are cooked, pick them up one at a time with a fork, and peel them under running cold water.

Put them in a double boiler with a little butter and sprinkle with salt. Cook for about 45 minutes.

Do not slice the beets; cutting seems to allow some of the sweetness to escape.

A pressure cooker will give excellent results but not quite as good as our method above. Young beets will require about 2 minutes' cooking after the steam first appears.

Beet Soup

For this we use the old beets. Cook the beets in boiling water until tender. Remove the skins, slice, and put into blender. Add hot consommé and run for 1 minute. Put into pot and let boil for 10 minutes, add salt, 2 teaspoons of sugar, and 2 tablespoons of tarragon vinegar, preferably Crosse and Blackwell. Strain and serve.

SUMMARY

1. *Use Ruby Queen for early planting.*
2. *Use Red Ball for late planting.*
3. *Make many plantings. We use 6 planting dates.*
4. *Use soluble fertilizer in seed trench.*
5. *Thin the rows.*
6. *Mulch with salt-marsh straw or salt-marsh hay.*
7. *Pick when very small.*

Brussels Sprouts

Candlewood vegetable rating	40
Variety: Catskill	*Source:* Harris
Seed treatment	Captan
Size of plot	3 × 38 ft. — 114 sq. ft.
Rows planted	3 ft. apart
Number of rows	1
In the row 15 plants	30 in. apart
Number of plants	15
Seed required for 38 ft. of row	1 pkt.
Season	Oct. 17–Dec. 15

PLANTING SCHEDULE IN IPSWICH

Start in greenhouse	May 5
Transplant to flats	June 1
Transplant to garden	June 20
Ready for picking (one week after first frost)	about Oct. 17
Finish	about Dec. 15

---

*

Brussels sprouts do not generally rate high among the pleasures of eating. In fact, most people think they are not worth eating at all. With the Mystery Chef Method of cooking, however, the situation is entirely changed. They are delicious. They also have one big advantage: they are not hurt by frost and can be left standing in the garden until December 15. The buttons picked then are as good as those picked in October. We have found that frost actually improves the quality of Brussels sprouts. As a result, they are not picked until one week after there has been a frost severe enough to kill the beans. We have them about once every five days.

VARIETIES

We have tried the following with good results:

Variety	Quality
Catskill	Excellent
Long Island Improved	Good
Jade Cross	Good

Others tried:

Dobbies Exhibition
Suttons Fillbasket
Long Island Mammouth

The Catskill is an outstanding variety. The plants grow straight about 30 inches high and the stalk is covered with small buttons.

DIFFICULTIES

Three troubles may be encountered but can be easily taken care of.

Cutworms, which can be destroyed by Diazinon.
Cabbage worms, which can be destroyed by malathion.
Rabbits, which can be kept out by a fence.

PROCEDURE

The seed is started in the greenhouse on May 5, transplanted to flats about June 1, and transplanted to the garden on June 20. We grow a few extra plants so that there will be replacements if they are needed. Since cutworms last in Ipswich until about the middle of June, this late planting, June 20, will escape most of them. Using this planting date, we have lost only one plant per year to cutworms, whereas when we planted a month earlier we lost up to half the plants to cutworms.

This late planting has another very important advantage; it causes each plant to grow a full crop of the small buttons that are best for cooking. The earlier planting caused many of the buttons to grow too big or to grow so badly formed that they could not be used.

Before the plants are set in the garden, a hole should be dug for each one, a little deeper than seems necessary, and a half spadeful of garden compost should be mixed into the soil at the bottom. If the plants do not start growing again soon after they are set out, then a soluble fertilizer should be used on them.

Immediately after setting the plants in the garden, you should start action against the cabbage worms and the few straggling cutworms that may still be around. The ground is sprayed with Diazinon, and the plants are sprayed with malathion.

As soon as the plants reach a height of 8 to 10 inches, set up a strong pipe at each end of the row and in the center, and stretch a wire along the pipes. Set a stake at each plant and tie it to the wire. This arrangement makes strong supports that will last until you take them apart. The plants should be tied to the stakes as soon as they are high enough, about 12 inches tall, since they need support if they are not to fall over.

The lowest sprouts on each plant develop first, and if the leaves between the sprouts are removed, they will develop all the way up the stem. About the middle of September, or when the lower sprouts are beginning to reach eating size, pinch at the growing points on the top of each plant. This will cause the sprouts on upper plant to develop more rapidly.

A fence around the garden is a must. Otherwise, you might just as well give up all ideas of ever harvesting any Brussels sprouts; the rabbits will get them first.

As soon as the buttons start to form, the plants should be sprayed with malathion, and applications should be repeated according to the manufacturer's directions. This will keep the cabbage worm under control.

YIELDS

A single plant of Catskill has produced as many as 2 pounds of buttons, which is a high yield. The yield from 1 row is about 22 pounds.

WINTER USE

Brussels sprouts freeze well.

COOKING

The small size buttons are the best flavored, but all are good, even the tiny ½ inch buttons. The large buttons should have the coarse outer leaves stripped off and all should be carefully trimmed and washed.

Use the Mystery Chef Method and there will be no odors of cabbage.
 Wash the Brussels sprouts.
 Boil rapidly 2 quarts of water in a 3-quart enamel pot.
 Add 1 teaspoon of baking soda and then the sprouts.
 Cook for 3 minutes uncovered; it is important to leave uncovered.
 If water foams, skim off the foam and reduce heat.
 Strain off water and return the sprouts to pot.
 Have water boiling rapidly in another 3-quart metal or enamel pot.
 Add 3 tablespoons of salt to boiling water.
 Add this boiling salt water to the sprouts in the enamel pot.
 Cook for 8 minutes uncovered for young sprouts, longer for old.
 After cooking, strain the sprouts, and return to pot.
 Add butter and salt.

Serve on hot plates and pour over the sprouts melted butter with a very little lemon juice in it. The hotter they are served, the better. The buttons will look clean, fresh, and most appetizing. Catskill Brussels sprouts grown in your garden and cooked in this manner are among the most delicious vegetables available in winter. Even the Brussels sprouts bought in the market are excellent cooked by this method.

SUMMARY

1. *Use Catskill variety.*
2. *Start in greenhouse on May 5.*
3. *Use garden compost when planting in garden.*
4. *Transplant to garden on June 20.*
5. *Spray to control cabbage worm.*
6. *Pick 1 week after first frost.*

Carrots

Candlewood vegetable rating　70

Variety: Nantes　*Source:* Harris

Seed treatment	Red oxide of copper
Size of plot: Garden	7 × 38 ft. — 266 sq. ft.
Rows planted	1 ft. apart
Number of rows	7
Seed required for 100 ft. of row	1 oz.
Seed required for this bed with 266 ft. of row	3 oz.
Season	June 22–Dec. 1
For winter use	Process or freeze young carrots — results good

PLANTING SCHEDULE IN IPSWICH

Plant	Begin	Finish	Days to maturity	Quality %
April 15	June 22	Aug. 1	68	100
May 1	July 5	Aug. 1	65	120
May 1	July 5	Aug. 1	65	120
May 1	July 5	Aug. 1	65	120
June 10	Aug. 1	Sept. 1	59	120
July 8	Sept. 1	Oct. 15	55	110
July 16	Sept. 15	Dec. 1	54	90

Carrots picked when they are small are very pleasant; they are tender and sweet and have a characteristic springlike flavor. Enjoy them at their best.

VARIETIES

We have tried the following varieties with good results:

Variety	Quality
Nantes	Excellent
Golden Beauty	Good
Coreless Chantenay	Good
Tendersweet	Good
Pioneer	Good

Others tried:

Champion Scarlet Horn	Pariesen
New Red Intermediate	Imperator
Danvers Half Long	

Of these, we like Nantes best; it is by far the most delicious variety, tender and extremely sweet.

Although carrots are like beets, and what has been said about beets can be applied to carrots, nevertheless, it seems useful to give the details about carrots even if they are repetitious.

DIFFICULTIES

Cutworms, which can be destroyed by Diazinon.

Rabbits, which can be kept out by a fence.

The only real trouble we have had in growing carrots at Candlewood, similar to that we had with beets, was that we used to find a part of each row, and occasionally nearly a whole row, in which either the seeds did not germinate at all or, if they did, the plants soon died from damping-off when they were about 1 inch tall.

In the past we made, in addition to our regular plantings, many experimental plantings to obtain the answers to the following questions.

1. How could we obtain satisfactory germination?
2. How can we prevent damping-off?

1. Germination

We believe that poor germination is due to one or more of the following conditions.

Planting too early. We have found at Candlewood that planting before April 1 was a complete failure. Practically none of the seeds survived, no matter what variety we used or what treatment we gave them. Of the seeds planted on April 10, about one-half survived. Seeds planted on April 15 or later gave completely satisfactory results if treated as later described. Probably every garden has its own critical dates, and these must be determined. The few seeds that did survive were planted on April 1 and bore by June 25. This is only five days earlier than the seeds planted on April 15.

As a result of these experiments, we settled on April 15 for the earliest planting in the garden.

Too much manure. Our garden is divided into two halves; what is grown one year on one half is grown on the other the next year. We found that we obtained an immediate improvement in germination if we did not use manure in the area in which the carrots were to be planted. This area did receive manure the following year when other crops were planted in it.

For the last few years, however, we have been using garden compost each year. In the fall the compost is spread over the garden and then worked into the soil with a rototiller. This procedure is excellent and is particularly good for the small-sized carrot seeds. We find it much better than using manure every other year.

Not enough lime. Our soil tested pH 6.1. We added enough ground limestone to bring the soil to pH 6.5 and tried again and found there was an improvement.

Damping-off

This is a term applied to the decay of young seedlings at or near the surface of the ground. The trouble is due to the action of various organisms. Sometimes, when the little plants were about 1 inch tall, a part of a row or, on occasions, a whole row would suddenly die. You can't then replant and have the row mature at the desired time. It is too late, and you won't have carrots when you want them. We tried a number of remedies and finally came to the decision to coat the seeds with red oxide of copper. This worked exceedingly well except when the ground was wet; it then became necessary to pregerminate the seeds and coat them with the red oxide.

PROCEDURE

As a result of many experiments, we used the following procedure, which worked satisfactorily:

1. In the plot where the carrots are to be planted, we use compost each year.

2. To prevent damage from cutworms, we sprayed the unplanted ground with Diazinon (carbaryl) in the early spring, and worked the spray in to 4 to 6 inches.

3. In the fall, the plot to be planted is tested for acidity, and enough ground limestone is added to bring the soil to pH 6.5.

4. We make a small trench in which the seeds are to be planted and apply 5–10–10 to the trench.

5. Because the soil of the garden at Candlewood is usually wet at the first planting, April 15, and sometimes at the second, the seedlings tend to damp-off. We have found that pregerminating the seeds and coating them with red copper oxide completely overcomes this trouble. It is a nuisance to do this, but if we want early carrots it is the only way we can have them. At that, it is a lot better to take this trouble and have the carrots rather than simply plant the carrot seeds only to discover that most of the seedlings are killed. We use the following procedure for pregermination.

a. Obtain a sieve with a wire screen that is just fine enough to prevent the carrot seeds from passing through. We have found that an 18-mesh screen is satisfactory for the varieties we use. Obtain some very fine sand, and screen enough to fill a glass.

b. Soak the carrot seeds in warm water for 8 hours.

c. Strain the seeds from the water.

d. Mix the seed with the screened sand and let stand for ½ hour. The dry sand will absorb the water from the seeds.

e. Put the mixture of seeds and sand in the sieve. The sand will pass through and leave the dry seeds in the sieve. The wet seeds are very difficult to sow and this is an easy way to overcome the difficulty.

f. Coat the seeds with red copper oxide. Put a teaspoon of the copper in a pint jar, add the seeds, and shake.

This method has worked well at Candlewood for many years and has prevented the bare patches in the early rows that we used to have. As soon as the ground is dry, pregerminating of the seed is not necessary; dusting the seeds with red copper oxide is sufficient.

6. Because carrot seeds are small, they are difficult to sow. Either too few or, what is more common, too many seeds are planted. Then thinning the rows later becomes a very tedious task. The use of a seed sower will greatly reduce the labor of thinning.

Plant the seeds, cover them with loam, firm them down, and sprinkle with water if dry. This method makes all the seeds germinate, and there is a little quick fertilizer to give them a good start.

The rows are all thinned so that the carrots are about 2 inches apart. In this way they grow quickly, are not misshapen from crowding, and all those in a row mature at about the same time. Inasmuch as there are not many in a row, those of one planting are generally eaten before the next planting matures.

7. We use salt-marsh straw or hay as a mulch on the carrot bed. The mulch is certainly worth using, for hardly a weed is seen and the quality of the carrots is improved. As with growing beets, this practice repays for the slight expense.

YIELDS

There is not much point in talking about yields when you intend to pick the carrots when they are one-quarter to one-half grown. But that is the time to pick them if you want the best carrots you ever tasted. The 7 rows we plant give us all the carrots we can use. Of these 7 rows, 2 rows are set aside for processing, or freezing if you prefer. The two rows give us 30 pint jars of carrots, which are enough to supply us with carrots for the winter. After Christmas, the quality falls off slightly, but they are still acceptable for eating in April.

WINTER USE

Storing. It is my belief that it is not worth eating stored carrots. They get poorer and poorer in quality and completely lose their eye appeal.

Freezing. Carrots freeze well for use in stews and casseroles.

Processing. Use only the early carrots planted May 1. Pick them while they are still very small, under 1 inch in diameter, and you can enjoy good carrots all winter.

COOKING

There is much talk about young spring carrots, but actually they are not ready to pick in this part of the world, that is, Ipswich, Massachusetts, until the latter part of June. When they do appear, however, they are decidedly tasty.

Buttered Carrots. Scrub the carrots with a brush until the skin comes off (this is better and easier than paring), cut into small pieces, parboil until tender, about 20 to 25 minutes, with just enough water to cover the carrots, and add a little salt. Drain, add melted butter and salt, and serve.

Carrots Glacé. Scrub the carrots with a brush until the skin comes off and parboil for 6 minutes. Don't cut up the carrots. Put them in a pot, add butter, sugar, and fresh mint leaves, and cook for 15 minutes. The smaller the carrots, the better they taste. Carrots no larger than ½ inch are just right.

Carrot Soup. This is a most delicious soup and very easy to make, provided a blender is available. To make 1 pint of soup, enough for 3 people, cut up and boil 3 medium-sized carrots and 1 onion (preferably a shallot) with enough water to cover until tender. Takes about 10 minutes. Cool.

Put carrots and onion, and the water in which they were boiled, into the blender. Add 1 cup of milk, run until the vegetables are thoroughly broken up (about 5 minutes), add 1 cup of cream, salt and pepper, and run for 1 minute more. Put in a double boiler and warm. Add chopped parsley when serving.

SUMMARY

1. *Use Nantes variety.*
2. *Make many plantings.*
3. *Fertilize seed trench.*
4. *Thin the rows and eat thinnings.*
5. *Mulch with salt-marsh straw or hay.*
6. *Pick when very young.*

Cauliflower

Candlewood vegetable rating   75

Varieties: Snowball	*Source:* Harris
Purple Head	*Source:* Harris

Seed treatment	Captan
Size of plot: Frame, 14 plants	6 × 4 ft. = 24 sq. ft.
Garden	6 × 38 ft. = 228 sq. ft.
Seed required: Snowball	1 pkt.
Purple Head	½ oz.
Season: Spring	June 5–June 25
Summer	July 1–Sept. 20

PLANTING SCHEDULE IN IPSWICH

	Start in green- house	Trans- plant to flat	Trans- plant to hot- frame	Sow in garden	Mature	Finish
Snowball	Feb. 20	Mar. 4	Apr. 1		June 5	June 25
Purple Head				Apr. 1	July 1	Aug. 1
Purple Head				May 8	July 20	Aug. 10
Purple Head				May 24	Aug. 10	Sept. 10
Purple Head				June 4	Sept. 1	Sept. 20

VARIETIES

At Candlewood, we grow a variety called Snowball in the hotframe. It is pure white, tender, very sweet, and of the highest quality. Over the years that we have been growing cauliflower, we have never had a failure.

We also grow a variety called Purple Head in the garden. The head has a lovely purple color and looks and tastes very much like broccoli. This is a little-used variety and should be tried.

DIFFICULTIES

None to date.

PROCEDURE

Sow and transplant on time.

In the spring, as soon as the plants have started to grow, spray with Diazinon and repeat, following label directions.

When the heads of the Snowball variety in the hotframe are about 2 inches in diameter, bend the big leaves over, tie them together with twine, and snap the leaf stems so that the leaves will shade and blanch the heads.

WINTER USE

Freeze.

COOKING

Delicious served raw with cocktails.

In the spring, cook when very small, not over 4 inches in diameter, and you will have something delicate and very sweet. These baby heads are not at all like the large cauliflower heads you buy in the market. In fact, the little baby heads, when covered with butter, are so sweet that you must be careful not to eat too many since they are very rich.

Use the Mystery Chef Method and there will be no odors.
  Wash the cauliflower.
  Boil rapidly 2 quarts of water in a 3-quart enamel pot.

Add 1 teaspoon of baking soda and then the cauliflower.
Cook for 3 minutes uncovered; it is important to leave
　uncovered.
If water foams, skim off the foam and reduce heat.
Strain off water and return cauliflower to pot.
Have water boiling rapidly in another 3-quart metal or
　enamel pot.
Add 3 tablespoons of salt to boiling water.
Add this boiling salt water to the cauliflower in the
　enamel pot.
Cook for 8 minutes uncovered for young cauliflower,
　longer for old.
After cooking, strain the cauliflower, and return to pot.
Add butter and salt.
The hotter it is served, the better.

In winter, when good fresh vegetables are few and far between,
you can have one of the most delicious dishes you have ever
enjoyed. For four people, use two heads of cauliflower. Cut the
heads into pieces about 2 inches square, wash and cook for 3
minutes in soda and 5 minutes in the salt water. The cauliflower
will thus be not completely cooked. Put the pieces in an open,
deep Pyrex dish.

Have ready a cream sauce made as follows:

> 1 chopped shallot sautéed in
> 2 tablespoons butter, add
> 2 tablespoons flour
> ½ teaspoon salt

Stir until well blended (about 2 minutes) and add 2 cups of
cream and a little grated cheese. Add this cream sauce to the
cauliflower in Pyrex dish and stir. Cover with grated cheese and
paprika. Bake for 10 minutes at 350°.

This is so good that, while it is enough for four people, it is very
easy for two people to eat every bit.

Celery

Candlewood vegetable rating 70

Variety: Summer Pascal
(Tall Fordhook)   *Source:* Harris

Seed treatment	None
Size of plot	16 × 38 ft. = 608 sq. ft.
Trenches planted	3 or 4 ft. apart
No. of rows (4 beds each of 2 rows)	8
In the row 41 plants	11 in. apart
Total number of plants	41 × 8 = 328 plants
Seed required for 304 ft. of row	2 pkts.
Yield of celery for this planting	328 bunches
Yield of celery for 100 ft.	107 bunches
Season	Oct. 10 through Jan. 1
For winter use	Leave in ground and cover

PLANTING SCHEDULE IN IPSWICH

Start in greenhouse	March 15
When seedlings are 1 in. high, transplant	about April 10
Transplant to garden	about June 1
After the first frost, ready to eat	about October 10

---

*

Celery is a delightful vegetable. We generally like to have it with a glass of cold milk; first a bite, then a sip of milk. One seems to enhance the other.

There is considerable difference in quality among varieties of celery, about the same as there is among kinds of corn. Furthermore, there is also a tremendous difference between the coarse outside stalks and the inner stalks. We happen to believe that only the inner part is worth eating; so our struggle is to produce enough hearts.

It is generally said that the outer stalks can be used for soup. Enjoying vegetables as we do, our family wants two hearts per person per meal; consequently, there would be enough outside stalks to provide soup for a restaurant. We have, therefore, grown the celery close together, which produces smaller plants; they have the same size hearts but fewer outside stalks.

VARIETIES

We have tried the following variety of celery with good results:

Variety	Quality
Summer Pascal (Tall Fordhook)	Excellent

Others tried:

Boston Market	Easy Blanching
White Plume	Utah
Golden Self-Blanching	Supreme Golden
Golden Plume	Colorado Pascal
Golden Phenomenal	Giant Pascal
Early Forcing	Cornell 19
Emperor	Salt Lake
Burpee's Fordhook	Solid White

Many of these varieties were obtained from different growers. We tried Pascal, which came from a planting of superexcellent quality; unfortunately, our planting did not compare favorably with the original. We obtained seeds from a Colorado farm that produced Pascal celery of the highest quality, but the plants did not do well at Candlewood. This would again support the belief, previously expressed, that each garden has its own set of conditions and that the best varieties for any piece of ground can be found only by experimenting. Of all the varieties tried, Boston Market was the best of the lot for quality, but was very susceptible to blight. Unfortunately, it is no longer available. Summer Pascal (Tall Fordhook) is excellent in quality and very resistant to blight.

DIFFICULTIES

Quite often, during the first few years that we grew celery, we discovered that about two or three weeks after the celery plants had been transplanted to the garden, they stopped growing for a considerable period. When they did start growing again, they never grew as well, nor was the quality as good as those that had not been checked. We experimented with manure water and found that, if it was applied about 7 days after the plants had been set out, and used twice more at 10-day intervals, the plants did well. Because manure water was a nuisance, we tried soluble fertilizer and found that the celery grew as well. It is truly extraordinary to see how quickly the plants grow and how readily they respond to this treatment. From the time we started using this method of feeding, we have never again had that trouble.

Another cause of trouble has been the blight. This, of course, is enough, because when it does come only a little of the whole crop can be harvested, and it is poor in quality. There does not seem to be any garden trouble worse than this. It is particularly exasperating because you start the seedlings in March, transplant them to flats, and finally set them out in the garden. Along about the middle of July, you see the poor things start to turn brown; then you know you are licked.

We used Boston Market for years, but, all of a sudden, the blight appeared and we lost nearly the entire crop. The following year, we tried some of the varieties that seemed promising, and that is no mean feat. When you read the catalogs, each variety is so outstanding and so good and so free from disease, it seems as if the sappiest sap could grow celery successfully. But try to do it.

PROCEDURE

The celery trenches are dug 5 feet apart, center to center, each trench 16 inches wide and 4 inches deep. The soil is thrown between the trenches and is smoothed over. Then compost is spread in the trenches about 2 inches thick; it is forked in well, making the finished trench about 2 inches below the surface. Then 2 pounds of 5–10–10 fertilizer, or 1 pound per 20 feet, is spread in each trench and raked in.

The celery plants, which have been started in the greenhouse, are planted in the trenches in 2 staggered rows 12 inches apart. The plants are set 11 inches apart in each row, thus giving 41 plants in each row. In the celery bed with 2 rows in each of the 4 trenches, there will be room for 328 plants, which will provide ample celery all winter.

As soon as the plants are set in the ground, they are sprayed with maneb or captan every week to 10 days throughout the growing season.

The celery is blanched by mounding the earth around the plants until finally, when the celery is full grown, the celery rows are 18 inches high and only the green tops are seen. We start picking one week after the first frost.

It is essential to keep the celery growing after you have set out the plants in the trenches. If the plants stop growing for any length of time, they are not likely to produce a good crop. About 7 days after planting, fertilize the plants with a soluble fertilizer (13–26–13) at 10-day intervals.

We have found celery an excellent crop and have had no trouble with it besides the blight. It takes considerable work to raise celery and a sizable amount of space in the greenhouse and coldframes, but the effort is not wasted.

Blanching celery can be accomplished in several ways, as follows:

a. Use of self-blanching varieties.
b. Putting paper cuffs on each bunch.
c. Tying boards on end along the celery rows.
d. By earthing.

Of these, the earthing method seems to give the best flavor and also has the advantage of protecting the plants against frost.

YIELDS

The area, 16 x 38 feet, that we use for celery produces 328 bunches of celery. This is a very large amount for one family to use, but we enjoy it so much that not a bunch remains.

STORING

There are several methods for storing celery grown in home gardens. We tried storing it in a root cellar but had poor results for several years and, after several experiments, gave up this method. Our failure to store celery successfully may have been due to a poor root cellar or to a lack of knowledge. In any event, we failed, so we tried leaving it where it grew in the garden. We have had success with this method for many years.

Late in the fall, about the end of November, we heap up the soil around the celery until only the heads show. We then cover the rows with straw both on the sides and over the tops; then we place galvanized corrugated iron sheets over the straw, one on each side and one over the top. The whole row is covered like a tent and no rain can enter.

If the ground is protected in this way, it remains dry and will not freeze. There is no difficulty in digging celery any time you want it during the winter. Simply shovel the snow out of the way, push the iron sheets along the row, and you can easily uncover as much celery as you wish to dig. We have found that celery so protected will keep better than that which we stored in the root cellar.

COOKING

Braised celery for four people can be prepared as follows:

Only the inside part of a bunch of celery should be used. Take 8 bunches and peel off the outer layers until the part of each bunch remaining is 1 to 1½ inches in diameter. Put this in a skillet and add only enough water to reach halfway to the top of the celery. Add a little salt, and cook until the celery is tender enough for a fork to prick it easily.

Strain off the liquid.

Dry the celery in a towel and roll it in a little flour.

Put ¾ of a tablespoon of butter in a frying pan and sear the celery in the butter until the celery is brown all over.

Put a can of Campbell's consommé in a saucepan and boil it down to half its original volume. Add it to the celery with salt, pepper, and a tablespoon of Kitchen Bouquet. Cook until very tender, about 20 minutes. It is so good, you should serve it as a separate course.

SUMMARY

1. *Use Summer Pascal variety.*
2. *Start in greenhouse.*
3. *Transplant to flats.*
4. *Transplant to garden.*
5. *Use several applications of soluble fertilizer.*
6. *Earth up.*
7. *Cover with straw and corrugated iron sheets for winter use.*

Corn

Candlewood vegetable rating 97

Varieties: Seneca 60	*Source:* Robson
Sugar and Gold	*Source:* Agway
Seneca Chief	*Source:* Robson

Seed treatment	Captan
Rows planted	3 ft. apart
Number of rows	16
Size of plot: Coldframe	6 × 38 ft. = 228 sq. ft.
Garden	45 × 38 ft. = 1710 sq. ft.
Seed required for 100 ft. of row	½ lb.
Seed required for this bed with	
608 ft. of row: Seneca 60	1 lb.
Sugar and Gold	½ lb.
Seneca Chief	1 lb.
Season: Coldframe	July 17–July 25
Garden	July 23–Oct. 10
For winter use	Freeze — Good

PLANTING SCHEDULE AT CANDLEWOOD

Variety	Planting dates	No. rows	Maturing dates	Days to mature	Comparative quality
Seneca 60	Apr. 22	2	July 17	86	100 (frame)
Seneca 60	May 1	1	July 23	83	110 (garden)
Sugar and Gold	May 15	1	July 28	74	110
Sugar and Gold	May 29	1	Aug. 5	68	115
Sugar and Gold	June 10	1	Aug. 12	63	115
Seneca Chief	May 27	2	Aug. 19	84	130 (freeze)
Seneca Chief	June 8	1	Aug. 26	79	130
Seneca Chief	June 17	1	Sept. 2	77	130
Seneca Chief	June 24	1	Sept. 9	77	130
Seneca Chief	June 28	1	Sept. 16	80	120
Seneca 60	July 3	2	Sept. 23	82	120
Seneca 60	July 8	1	Sept. 30	84	110
Seneca 60	July 11	1	Oct. 4	85	100

For the purpose of comparing the quality of corn at the different seasons, the earliest corn, Seneca 60, was called 100 and the test compared to it. From the table, it is seen that Sugar and Gold is a little better and Seneca Chief still better. As the season advances, the quality of Seneca 60 becomes poorer.

Corn, in our opinion, is second only to asparagus so far as the pleasure of eating is concerned — a very close second at that, for what can be nicer than good corn with enough butter? Of all the vegetables, none deteriorates in quality as fast as corn. Corn of the best quality simply cannot be obtained in the markets or even at the best restaurants. If you want good corn, you must select the best varieties, grow it yourself, and eat it a few hours after picking. Corn that is two or three days old, as it generally is when sold in the markets, is only about 15 percent as good as the best quality.

Much has been written about the necessity to delay picking the corn until just before you are ready to cook it. Although we had accepted this dictum, we were not convinced of its validity. To satisfy ourselves, we cooked four lots of corn. We ate these with the following results:

No. hours cut before eating	Quality (%)
2	100
8	75
26	50
50	0

Several trials were made, so that the results are accurate. From this table it appears that, for every hour after cutting, the corn loses 2 percent of its sweetness and becomes proportionately tougher. Since the corn was very uniform, we used 3 ears for each cutting or 12 ears per person for each tasting. In four tastings, we used 96 ears for two people. It does take up a surprising amount of garden space to conduct such tests, and 12 ears of corn make a large order for each person to sample. Much of the corn now sold in the markets is put in cold rooms and carried to market in refrigerated trucks, with the result that the quality is better than it used to be. However, in the markets it is still held at room temperature, so that in 8 hours it loses at least one-quarter of its quality.

VARIETIES

The market people cannot know the names of the corn they sell, for they buy it from different sources. Often you will see corn marked Golden Bantam and the corn will be no more Golden Bantam than Black Mexican. Unless you know the actual grower, you cannot be sure of the correct name. If you purchase some so-called Golden Bantam and compare it with other varieties, don't be surprised if you are disappointed in the results.

Corn has the great advantage of having a very long season — in Ipswich, it runs from July 17 to October 10 — whereas, in comparison, asparagus lasts only from May 1 to June 22.

We have tried the following varieties:

Varieties	*Quality*
Seneca 60, Earliest	Excellent
Sugar and Gold, Early	Excellent
Seneca Chief, Main Crop	Excellent
Aunt Mary (White)	Good
Golden Bantam	Good
Carmel Cross	Good
Cream-O-Gold	Good
Early Pearl	Good
Early Sensation	Good
Golden Cross Bantam	Good
Harvard Hybrid	Good
Ioana	Good
Wonderful	Good

Other varieties tried:

Butter and Sugar	King's Crest	Priscilla
Dwarf	Lee	Spring Gold
Early Market	Luther Hill	Sprite
Flagship	Marcross	Sugar Sweet
Gold Mine	Mexican Black Seeded	Sweet Sue
Golden Gem	North Star	Tender Gold
Golden Sunshine	Northern Belle	Yellow Tangerine
Hickory King	Plymouth	

and 44 varieties of unnamed hybrids.

As a result of the trials of about 90 varieties carried on since 1930, the following 3 varieties have been selected.

Seneca 60. Of all the extremely early varieties that we have tried, this is the only one we consider of sufficiently good quality to grow. The stalks are about 5 feet tall and the ears, 2 per stalk, are small, $6\frac{1}{2}$ to 7 inches long. It is very hardy and stands early planting. The quality is excellent, but its greatest asset is that it is very early. We use it also as a late corn. It matures faster than Seneca Chief, and for that reason is better suited for late planting. The longer maturing corn, when planted late, sometimes does not mature if the weather is a little colder than average. Seneca 60 does not grow as tall as Seneca Chief, and is less likely to be destroyed by high winds.

Sugar and Gold. The reason for growing this variety is its quality, rated as excellent, which is better than that of Seneca 60. If the seeds are planted at the same time as Seneca 60, on April 10 and May 1, they will not germinate in the cold ground; planted on May 15 or later, when the ground is warm, all the seeds will germinate.

The stalks are only $4\frac{1}{2}$ feet tall — almost a midget corn — and the ears are about 5 inches long and $1\frac{3}{4}$ inches in diameter. They contain mostly yellow kernels with a few white ones mixed among them. It is a good corn to grow.

Seneca Chief. This is of excellent quality and is the best corn we have tried. The stalks grow very tall, up to 9 feet. The ears are of perfect size, about 7 inches long and $1\frac{3}{4}$ inches in diameter, and uniform in appearance and quality. The yield is very high. Although they are tender and sweet, the kernels are hard to remove from the cob. The ears do not all mature at the same time, so that from each row there is a picking season of about 8 days.

Many people claim they prefer white corn simply because of the color, but if you were blindfolded, it is unlikely that you could tell them apart. Theoretically, at least, you should select the corn that is the best regardless of its color. Nearly all our experiments have been limited to yellow corn because it is usually of better quality, higher yield, and is far easier to eat than white corn, with its irregular kernels.

Remember, in comparing corn, that the corn samples should all be picked at the same time and eaten at the same time. Because corn will deteriorate within a few hours, it is obviously unfair to buy corn in the market and compare it with corn picked and eaten soon after. Most of the corn sold in supermarkets is at least 48 hours old, and the quality has been ruined.

For the three varieties of corn that we grow, it takes about 8 days between the time the corn in a particular row is just right to pick and the day the last corn in that row reaches the same degree of maturity. Therefore, the rows should be planted so that they will mature about 7 or 8 days apart. If the rows mature more quickly than 8 days apart, you won't be able to use all the good corn, and some of it will grow too old to eat. If the rows mature more than 8 days apart, you will be without good corn. If we want a continuous supply of good corn at its best, with each row maturing at just the right moment, it is necessary to make 13 plantings.

The first planting is made on April 22 in a permanent wood coldframe. The frame is high enough to let the corn grow to a height of about 15 inches before the glass must be removed. This date is desirable, for you can obtain corn about 6 days before that grown in the open garden. The last planting is a gamble in Ipswich. About once in four years it is destroyed by frost, but some years the corn lasted until October 26.

It is interesting to note how the quality varies with the season. Of course, when the first corn comes in, it always is exciting, but it really is not as good as that which comes later. By the end of September, corn is no novelty and, perhaps, you become a little too critical. Corn planted on July 8 has always borne good ears, except when they were killed by frost, but at least three ears should be cooked for every two eaten. One in three is likely to be not quite ripe enough.

In Ipswich, the ears of the first planting are ripe 18 days after tassels appear on half of the corn stalks in the row.

In 1946, we were given a collection of hybrid seeds to plant all at one time; they were to mature at different dates. These we planted on May 13 and they matured as follows:

Seed no.	Maturity	Quality (%)
1	July 30	60
2	July 30	100
3	Aug. 11	90
4	Aug. 16	80
5	Aug. 19	60
6	Sept. 7	60

As far as maturing on succeeding dates over a long period, it was an extraordinarily good selection of seeds, and as a research job it was important. Right away the question arises: Why not plant only No. 2 and have the highest quality all summer?

This test convinced us that the idea of making plantings of several different varieties at one time, so that you can obtain a succession of corn all summer, is misleading and fallacious for the following reasons:

First, you do not save any time or labor by planting all at once. Any given number of rows of corn will require the same total hours of labor if they are planted at one time or at several times.

Second, it will take considerable experimentation to find several varieties that will produce mature rows of corn at exactly the number of days apart that you want.

Third, if you finally find several varieties that mature as you wish them to, you will then discover that one variety is better than the others. Why not plant that one on different dates? What you really want is the best corn you can raise. Many kinds of corn that appear on given dates like a timetable may be interesting, but it is not what you should really want.

Comparing different varieties of corn is not the easiest thing to do. To pick the best quality corn, a number of varying qualities must be taken into account, such as:

> Flavor.
> Size of cob.
> Size of kernels.
> Regularity of the kernel rows.
> Ease of separating the kernels from the cob.
> Tenderness or toughness of the kernels.
> Texture of kernels.
> Time required to ripen.

In addition to these there are other characteristics to be considered, such as size of plants, yields, and susceptibility to disease.

In selecting the varieties finally chosen, all these qualities were taken into consideration and each variety qualifies as best for its season.

DIFFICULTIES

In Ipswich, there are no high winds to knock down the early corn, but all corn maturing after September 1 has to be supported. The earth should be pushed up around the base of corn, thus making a succession of small hills that will help support the corn stalks.

Then we place pipes in the corn rows before the corn is fully grown and stretch one wire about 4 feet off the ground. A piece of string is tied to one of the end pipes and then about every 4 feet along the wire, thus fastening the corn between the wire and string. This is enough to support the corn in even the highest winds. It may seem a little troublesome to do this, but if you ever saw 6 or 8 of your corn rows, which are supposed to supply you for the last four weeks of the season, lying flat on the ground, you would never hesitate about tying up the corn. It will give you a certain sense of satisfaction and security to see the corn standing in rows nicely tied to the wire.

Until 1947, we had had no corn borers or earworms, but in that year they descended on us in hordes. Although little damage was done to the early corn, we lost all the late corn — about two-fifths of the crop. This was a major catastrophe and something had to be done. The next year we started spraying with DDT with promising results. At the end of the year we found that we had not sprayed enough, either in amount or in the number of sprays. Since DDT, for better or worse, is no longer available, we now use a time schedule of spraying with Sevin (carbaryl) and Diazinon.

PROCEDURE

Some of the corn seed sold today is treated with chemicals by the companies that sell it. If the seed we buy is not treated, we do so ourselves with captan. The corn and the captan are put in a glass bottle and shaken up. This is very easy to do and takes only a few minutes.

Corn is generally planted in rows with the seeds 8 to 18 inches apart; the distance usually recommended is 12 inches. We plant much closer than that. In planting the seed, we take a hoe and make a depression every 24 inches about 10 inches wide and 12 inches long and 1½ inches deep. The soil from each depression is always pulled in one direction. Six seeds of corn are then sowed, one in each corner and two in the center about 3 inches apart. The soil is then pulled back into the depression and tamped down with the flat side of the hoe. Planting 6 seeds every 24 inches gives 3 seeds per foot, or three times as much as is generally recommended. Planting such as this may well be criticized as being too close, but the fact remains that we do have corn of good quality and of good yield.

Each 38-foot row produces the following number of good ears, that is, excluding those too small to eat.

	Ears per row	Ears per foot of row
Earliest corn	45	1.2
Early corn	50	1.3
Main corn	66	1.7
Late corn	50	1.3

For early corn, use permanent coldframes. These should be 12 inches high in front, 18 inches high in back, and 6 feet wide. Unless these are as high as specified, the corn will grow so tall that it will hit the glass and be damaged by the late frosts. As soon as all danger of frost is over, the glass frames can be removed and the corn allowed to grow as if no frame were there. The frame should be at one end of the garden and across the entire width of the garden so that the early corn is planted in the part of the frame on the corn side of the garden; the early peas are planted in the frame on the other side of the garden. After the early peas have been harvested, corn is planted in the same frame with the glass sash removed, thus using the same frame twice. The wood sides do no harm.

WINTER USE

We freeze the corn on the cob. In the first place — and it is most important, we believe — this method produces the finest-flavored corn. In the second place, also very important, this is the easiest way to freeze corn. Cutting the kernels off a large quantity of corn

direct from the garden is hard and tedious. Then, too, it takes a
long time, because the kernels do not come off easily. It is much
simpler to freeze the whole ear.

1. We use a large pot of 24-quart capacity. This is filled
nearly full of water and set boiling as rapidly as possible on two
burners. The more heat available, the better. Into this pot put
15 ears of corn. This will cool the water, but with the large
volume the temperature will remain high. As soon as the water
starts to boil again, the time is noted and the corn is boiled for
only 2 minutes. This is called blanching.

2. The ears are cooled under running water.

3. They are then picked up and dried with a towel, laid in a
flat pan, and placed in the freezer until they are almost frozen.
This is a very quick way to reduce their temperature.

4. When they are almost frozen, the whole ears are put into
plastic bags, three to a bag. Tie the end of the bag, and put the
packages, spread out loosely, into the freezer. By spreading
them loosely, you will allow for circulation of air, and the ears
will freeze solid very quickly. When frozen solid, the packages
can be placed close together.

Speed is most essential. The most important thing is to freeze
every kernel in the shortest possible time, and you should do
everything you can to accomplish this.

The most important fact to remember in freezing corn, or
anything else for that matter, is that, since the frozen product is not
as good as the fresh product, only the very best should be used for
freezing. Look at each ear and ruthlessly discard the ears that are
not of the finest quality. Pick each ear for freezing as if you
yourself were planning to eat it at once. Ears for freezing should
be a little more mature than those picked for eating at once.

COOKING

Our method of cooking corn is certainly simple. Drop the ears into a large pot of rapidly boiling water for just 3 minutes. Good corn can be cooked in that short a time. More cooking will certainly lower its quality. If corn can't be cooked in that time, it is not of good quality and longer cooking won't help it.

Frozen corn, or at least corn frozen on the cob, should be cooked very differently. Put the corn directly from the freezer into a pressure cooker and cook for 1 minute at 15 pounds of pressure. Pick up the ears one at a time, and cool the little end of the cob under running cold water to give you something to hold on to, since the ears will be very hot. Then quickly cut the kernels, which are not yet completely cooked, off the cob and into a Pyrex dish. Add salt and butter and place under the broiler for a few minutes to finish cooking the corn. Serve piping hot. One minute in the pressure cooker is long enough for cooking the kernels but not nearly sufficient to heat the inside of the cob. Therefore cut the kernels off at once; otherwise they will become tepid and soggy. If the corn were cooked long enough to heat the inside of the cob, the kernels would be overcooked and spoiled. Even frozen corn on the cob bought in the markets is fairly good if cooked in this manner.

Seneca Chief picked at the right moment, frozen, and cooked in the manner described has a quality about the same as that of the earliest corn grown in the garden. The comparison was made when the Seneca 60 was first picked in the garden, at which time the Seneca Chief was about 11 months old.

There is always the question of how to eat corn, except for Seneca Chief. If it is cut off the cob in the kitchen, you can be sure that some ears, not of the best quality, will get mixed in, thus reducing the quality 10 to 15 percent. We enjoy picking out the ears that seem best to us as the corn is passed, and eating them on the cob. There is quite a difference in quality in a dozen ears of corn. If you want the best, you must be able to decide quickly when it is passed around. It is a funny thing, but many persons are helpless when it is their turn to choose which ear to eat. In any lot of corn that is passed to the table, there are two things to remember in selecting an ear. First, the ears with medium-sized kernels are best. Those with kernels too small are not ripe, and those with large kernels are too old. Pick an ear of medium color. The size of the kernel is the most important indication; if it is the right size, the color can be whitish or yellowish, but it will still be good, although the medium color is the best. If you want the best, remember that there should be at least three ears cooked for every two eaten. In that way, if you know how to select corn, you can be assured of the best.

Seneca Chief, however, is the exception to eating corn on the cob. Because the kernels stick rather tightly to the cob, they should be cut off the cob in the kitchen. If, from one lot of Seneca Chief that has been picked and cooked together, you will try some on the cob and some cut off the cob, you will notice quickly the better quality of the corn that has been cut off the cob.

Succotash, the mixture of corn and lima beans, that old standby, seems a distressing notion; you lose the best of both vegetables by mixing them. However, since it is used so much, there must be some good in it. Each to his own taste.

SUMMARY

1. *Use Seneca 60, Sugar and Gold, and Seneca Chief.*
2. *Plant in hills.*
3. *Use wire or pipes to protect late corn.*
4. *Make many plantings.*
5. *Spray frequently.*

Cucumbers

Candlewood vegetable rating 20

Variety: Marketer Source: Burpee

Seed treatment Captan
Size of plot 3 X 20 ft. = 60 sq. ft.
Rows planted ½
5 plants 4 ft. apart
Seed required for this bed
with 30 ft. of row 1 pkt.
Season July 18–Oct. 10

| PLANTING SCHEDULE IN IPSWICH | |
Plant in garden	Mature
May 1	July 18
May 25	Aug. 1
June 1	Aug. 5

Cucumbers we use but little — a few in salads and some on small rounds of bread, with a dab of homemade mayonnaise, with cocktails, and, occasionally, sliced cucumbers on ice with no dressing. These are delicious served without embellishment and are of a class apart from all other vegetables. They are so fresh and delicate that they remind one of dew early in the morning.

We have tried the following with good results:

Varieties	Quality
Marketer	Excellent
Challenger	Good

*

Others tried:

Cubit   Straight Pack
Farquhars Perfection   China
Victory   Straight 8
Davis Perfect   King of the Ridge
Forcing White Spine   Henderson Bush

DIFFICULTIES

Very few. Each year we have had good cucumbers.

PROCEDURE

A hole 15 inches in diameter and 3 inches deep should be scooped out where the hills are to be planted. A shovelful of garden compost should be worked into the hole and the soil returned. The seeds, ten to a hill, should be planted directly over the compost and then thinned later to five. It is amazing to see how the plants grow on compost. We spray very lightly for cucumber beetles with Diazinon or Sevin.

YIELDS

The five hills produce about 50 cucumbers, which is enough for our needs.

COOKING

We have tried cooking cucumbers in a number of ways, and none seems worth repeating.

SUMMARY

1. *Use Marketer variety.*
2. *Spray with Sevin.*

 Eggplant

Candlewood vegetable rating	30
Variety: Jersey King	*Source:* Burpee
Seed treatment	Captan
Size of plot	3 × 19 ft. = 57 sq. ft.
Rows planted	3 ft. apart
Number of rows	½
In the row 9 plants	2 ft. apart
Seed required	1 pkt.
Season	Aug. 3–Oct. 10

PLANTING SCHEDULE IN IPSWICH	
Start in greenhouse	Mar. 1
Transplant (when ¾ in. high)	about Mar. 12
Pot up in 3-inch pots	about Apr. 30
Transplant to garden	June 1
Expect to mature	Aug. 3

*

Eggplant is a rather pleasant vegetable to use, about once in five days. It has a peculiar biting flavor all its own, and there is no other vegetable with this characteristic.

VARIETIES

The standard variety, Black Beauty, is lovely to look at, but is rather too large in diameter. Jersey King, which is smaller in diameter, about 2½ inches, is of better size and quality. This variety is something like a cucumber in shape and is a beautiful vegetable, blackish purple with a glistening sheen.

We have tried the following varieties with good results:

Varieties	*Quality*
Jersey King	Excellent
Early Long Purple	Excellent
Black Beauty	Good

DIFFICULTIES

None.

PROCEDURE

To kill cutworms, spray the ground before planting with Diazinon.

The seedlings are set out on June 1 when the soil is thoroughly warm, because eggplant is extremely sensitive to frost. A hole is dug for each plant, about 6 inches deep, and a handful of garden compost is mixed into the soil at the bottom. If the plants do not start growing again soon after they are set out, then soluble fertilizer should be used.

As soon as the plants reach a height of 8 to 10 inches, a strong pipe should be placed at each end of the row and a wire run from one pipe to the other. Place a slender stake at each plant, and tie the stake to the wire. As the plants grow, they, in turn, are tied to the stakes. This arrangement provides strong support.

COOKING

Eggplant is very easy to cook and does not need the salting process so often recommended. Simply peel and cut the eggplant into slices about ¼ inch thick. Cover both sides with flour and sauté in olive oil. The flour will make a thin covering for the slices. If butter is used, the eggplant slices will burn.

SUMMARY

1. Use Jersey King variety.
2. Set stakes at each plant.

Fennel

Variety: Florence   *Source:* Burpee

Number of rows	2
Rows planted	1 ft. apart
Trench for the 2 rows	4 ft. apart
Seed required for 76 ft.	1 oz.
Season	Sept. 20–Dec. 1

PLANTING SCHEDULE IN IPSWICH

Start in greenhouse	April 13
Transplant to garden	June 25

This vegetable, although listed in many seed catalogs, is seldom seen growing in home vegetable gardens.

Fennel is very similar to celery but is easier to grow. The trench should be prepared with compost and then the seedlings set out about June 25. It grows beautifully, and there are no difficulties other than weeds. As they grow, the plants should be earthed up, as is done with celery.

We use fennel, cut like celery, with cocktails. It is pleasant and something of a novelty.

COOKING

To cook, place in a blender:
    1 cup milk
    2 fennel hearts
    1 tablespoon flour
    2 tablespoons butter
    1 teaspoon salt
Mix for 20 seconds. Add 1 cup milk. Mix 3 minutes.
    Cook in a double boiler. Strain.

Jerusalem Artichoke

Variety: Jerusalem	*Source:* Park
Seed treatment	None
Size of plot	25 sq. ft.
Rows planted	1
Tubers required	2 qts.
Season	Oct. 10–Jan. 10

PLANTING SCHEDULE IN IPSWICH

Plant in garden	Apr. 15
Mature	Sept. 10

This is an unimportant vegetable that we use very occasionally in the late fall when the summer garden is finished. If artichokes were not so easy to grow and so free from disease, it is unlikely that we should grow them. It is a pity there are not more vegetables as hardy as this one. Artichokes grow like weeds, with rather thin stalks that wave in the wind. The white edible tubers, grown like potatoes, are crisp and provide an interesting change in one's fare. They should not be planted in the garden, since they will spread, and they are difficult to eradicate once they have had a start in any piece of ground; rather they should have a little plot, to one side, all by themselves, protected from the winds.

PROCEDURE

We have tried only one variety that has been satisfactory. It is planted on April 15 and matures in September, but we do not use it until after the first heavy frost, about October 10. We have not had any difficulties and, apparently, it will grow under almost any conditions. The plants, which grow very tall and large, up to 8 feet high, bear single sunflowerlike blooms. One row 25 feet long gives us all we can use.

Let the roots remain in the ground, cover them with straw and a piece of galvanized corrugated steel, and you can dig them during the winter whenever you need them.

COOKING

We have four uses for Jerusalem artichokes:
1. Peel and serve with mayonnaise with cocktails.
2. Cook and use in salads.
3. Cook au gratin.
4. Boil and serve with Hollandaise sauce.

Lettuce

Candlewood vegetable rating 70

    Varieties: May King   *Source:* Chase
            Buttercrunch *Source:* Harris

Seed treatment	None
Size of hotframe	6 × 6 ft. = 36 sq. ft.
Size of garden plot	4 × 38 ft. = 152 sq. ft.
Rows planted: ½ row at a planting	1 ft. apart
In the rows plants	1 ft. apart
Number of rows (excluding frames)	4
Number of plantings (including frames)	19
Seed required for bed: May King	2 pkts.
Buttercrunch	3 pkts.
Season	May 1–Nov. 25

PLANTING SCHEDULE IN IPSWICH

	Variety	Sow in greenhouse	Set out	Bear	Finish
Hotframe	May King	Feb. 20	Mar. 25	May 1	June 4
Coldframe	May King	Feb. 20	Apr. 1	June 1	June 14
Garden	May King	Mar. 15	Apr. 15	June 12	June 22
	Buttercrunch	Mar. 31	May 6	June 22	July 4
	Buttercrunch	Apr. 12	May 16	June 30	July 14
	Buttercrunch	Apr. 22	May 25	July 8	July 18
	Buttercrunch	May 1	June 4	July 16	July 25
	Buttercrunch	May 7	June 12	July 24	Aug. 1
	Buttercrunch	May 14	June 22	Aug. 1	Aug. 8
	Buttercrunch	May 21	June 29	Aug. 9	Aug. 17
	Buttercrunch	May 28	July 5	Aug. 17	Aug. 25
	Buttercrunch	June 8	July 15	Aug. 25	Sept. 2
	Buttercrunch	June 15	July 24	Sept. 2	Sept. 10
	Buttercrunch	June 23	Aug. 3	Sept. 10	Sept. 18

	Variety	Sow in greenhouse	Set out	Bear	Finish
	Buttercrunch	July 2	Aug. 12	Sept. 18	Sept. 25
	Buttercrunch	July 12	Aug. 23	Sept. 26	Oct. 10
Coldframe	May King	July 20	Aug. 29	Oct. 10	Oct. 24
Coldframe	May King	Aug. 1	Sept. 10	Oct. 25	Nov. 14
Coldframe	May King	Aug. 8	Sept. 18	Nov. 10	Nov. 25

Some people prefer lettuce to any other vegetable. Many rate it as at least among the five best vegetables. In any event, if you can produce good lettuce, it is a most important vegetable. We use it practically every day from the beginning of the season, about May 1, until it is finished about December 25.

VARIETIES

We have tried the following varieties with good results:

Variety	Quality
May King	Excellent
Buttercrunch	Excellent
White Boston	Excellent
Black Seeded Tennis Ball	Good
Golden Ball	Good

Others tried:

All Head	Ideal	Slobolt
Bibb	Imperial 44	Summer Market
Cos Iceberg	Mammouth	Sutton
Crisp as Ice	Matchless	Tennis Ball Selected
Deacon	Mignonette	Tetue Deniens
Great Lakes	Oak Leaf	Winter Lettuce
Heartwell	Salad Bowl	White Paris Romaine
Iceberg	Salamander	Winner

We have tried 30 varieties of lettuce over the years. Undoubtedly, some of those that failed or did not do well would be excellent in other gardens. Each garden has its own conditions, and the variety best suited for it should be chosen after trial. As a result of our experiments, we now use only May King and Buttercrunch. The early May King lettuce, which grows in the cool spring weather, is the best of all, but Buttercrunch, a larger Butterhead variety, is excellent, even in summer.

As you will observe from the schedule, we have the first lettuce from the concrete hotframe about May 1; it lasts until June 4. Our particular hotframe is small so that we can grow only about 48 heads, but that is enough to give us a great deal of pleasure.

Asparagus and lettuce the first of May — how we look forward to that happy day. Then for five weeks, we have lettuce from the hotframe. It takes a little planning and some permanent equipment to accomplish this, but you will think it a very good investment if you once try it yourself.

DIFFICULTIES

We have had excellent results with lettuce. Our only real difficulty has been rabbit trouble, which was cured by a wire fence.

PROCEDURE

So often you hear garden owners say that in summer their lettuce goes to seed, and that all they can raise are the cabbagelike varieties that are poor in quality. At Candlewood, we grow good lettuce all summer by following a very simple rule: Make many plantings. In that way, no planting in the hot weather is expected to last longer than nine days after the heads in any one row have matured. A few in any row may go to seed, but there will still be plenty left. It certainly is a chore to start the seeds in the greenhouse, transplant once, and then plant in the garden, but it is the only way in which we have been able to grow good heading lettuce all summer, and we are able to enjoy it every single day.

Before arriving at this simple solution, we tried growing many so-called summer varieties, that is, kinds that do not go to seed in the hot weather. We also tried different methods of growing, such as using shade over the plants. It is true that we were able to grow lettuce of the Iceberg type, like Great Lakes, but it was not worth eating; it tasted more like cabbage than lettuce.

All our lettuce is started from seed in the greenhouse and transplanted. If a greenhouse is not available for starting your lettuce, buy flats of the varieties you like from a local grower, or arrange with some nearby greenhouse to start your own seeds for you.

The earliest planting is made in a hotframe, and an area equal to two sashes is used. In the fall the same two frames are used again but no heat is required.

In the garden, ½ row, or 18 feet, is planted at a time. Four rows will take care of 8 plantings. After the eighth planting is made, then the first row is replanted.

We use salt-marsh straw on the lettuce bed as a mulch. It insures good plant growth and improves the quality. We place it on the bed 3 inches deep when the lettuce plants are about 3 inches high and have started to send out their leaves. Every head in the row matures satisfactorily. It is always a pleasure to look at the lettuce bed, for there are rows of perfect heads resting on a light brown carpet of delightful appearance. By all means, use a mulch of salt-marsh straw or salt-marsh hay or peat moss.

YIELDS

We plant as shown on the chart on p. 118.

Theoretically this planting should yield 398 heads of lettuce, but some fail, some are destroyed, and some go to seed. To assure ourselves of about 300 heads (an average for the seven months of approximately 43 heads per month), we plant the number specified.

		No. heads
In the hotframe — 2 sashes	Spring	48
In the coldframe — ½ row	Spring	18
In the garden — 16 plantings	Spring	266
In the coldframe — ½ row	Fall	18
In the hotframe — 2 sashes (no heat used)	Fall	48
		398

This may seem like a lot of lettuce, yet if you want one head of lettuce available each and every day, then some must be wasted. With anything as easy to grow as lettuce, we deem it a good idea always to have plenty on hand.

SALADS

Over the years, we have discovered that we never tire of simple salads and can eat one every day. But from fancy salads deliver us! Our standard, everyday salad contains one or more of the following:

Beets   Persimmons
Carrots   Canned pear
Stringbeans   Alligator pear

with simple French dressing, for two people, made fresh each time, as follows:

Dissolve 1 teaspoon sugar in 1 tablespoon of white vinegar.
   Add 2 tablespoons of olive oil, salt, a few grains of cracked black pepper

or the following:

Tomatoes	Cooked celeriac
Cucumbers	Hard-boiled eggs
Jerusalem artichokes	Diced cooked chicken

with homemade mayonnaise, so easy to make in a blender, as follows:

Put in 2 egg yolks, ¼ cup olive oil, 1½ tablespoons of white wine vinegar, ¼ teaspoon dry mustard, ½ rounded teaspoon sugar, ¼ teaspoon salt.
Cover blender and turn on to low speed.
Stop, uncover, and at low speed pour in ¾ cup oil slowly.

This never curdles, makes 1¼ cups, and stores very well.

There are hundreds of different salad dressings, but one that provides a pleasant alternative to the above is Essex CMW. Although it is somewhat more elaborate, and perhaps more likely to disguise the taste of lettuce, we think it enhances a winter salad particularly well. You might even learn to enjoy spinach in a salad using this concoction:

Parboil one egg 1½ minutes. Place in jar and shake vigorously.
Add juice of one lemon, ¾ cup salad oil, 1 teaspoon salt, ½ teaspoon freshly ground pepper, one garlic clove chopped finely, ¼ cup grated cheese (Parmesan).
Again, shake vigorously.

Lima Beans

Candlewood vegetable rating 85

Variety: Fordhook 242 — Bush   *Source:* Burpee, Harris

Seed treatment	Captan
Rows planted	3 ft. apart
Number of rows	6
Size of plot	18 ft. × 38 ft. = 684 sq. ft.
Seed required	2 lbs.
For winter use	Freeze — Results excellent

PLANTING SCHEDULE IN IPSWICH

Plant in garden	June 1
Season	Aug. 10–Oct. 10

Lima beans have a vegetable rating of 85, fifth on the Candlewood rating list. They have good texture and a delicious flavor. Of all the different varieties of vegetables grown in the garden, lima beans are almost the last to mature. At first, you might think this late maturity a drawback, but actually it is not. Limas mature after the peas have finished, and although they cannot take the place of peas, nevertheless they have an attraction all of their own. At the end of the summer, it is certainly refreshing to have something as good as limas appear on the table and know that they can be picked until the first frost. They are not resistant to cold, and the first sign of frost is the end of the limas. At Candlewood, lima beans are free of disease and pests and are easy to grow.

VARIETIES

We have tried the following with good results:

	Variety	*Quality*
Bush:	Fordhook 242	Excellent
	Fordhook Concentrated	Good
Pole:	Dr. Harold Martin	Excellent
	Ideal	Good
	King of the Garden	Good
	Sieva	Good

Others tried:

Burpee's Improved Bush	Leviathan Pole
Henderson Bush	USDA 2

The Fordhook 242 is a bush lima with small, pale green beans of high quality. We use this variety because it matures early.

Although, in general, frozen vegetables are not as good as fresh ones, this variety of bean when frozen is, of all the varieties of frozen vegetables that we have tried, the nearest to fresh. The frozen limas in late winter and spring are delicious. You wouldn't want a better vegetable; in fact, we grow 2 rows just for freezing. Lima beans should be picked while still young; old ones are not worth eating.

DIFFICULTIES

Cutworms are destroyed by treating the unplanted soil with Diazinon.

Mexican bean beetles are destroyed by Sevin.

Rabbits are very fond of young limas and can eat the tops off a whole row of young plants in one night. Wire fencing around the entire garden is the only protection.

PROCEDURE

For the Fordhook 242 variety, a trench 4 inches wide and 2 inches deep is made in a V shape. The seeds are sown 8 inches apart, covered with soil, and firmed down. If the seeds are planted closer, there is likely to be so much leaf growth that the sun can't get in, and, as a consequence, the beans will be delayed in maturing and the yield will be very poor. When we plant snap beans, we wet the trench with water, but we have learned that the lima seeds do better without water.

When the plants are 4 inches high, the ground should be mulched 3 inches thick with salt-marsh straw. If this is not available, salt-marsh hay or peat moss can be used.

When the plants start to leaf out, we dust with Sevin to kill the Mexican bean beetles. The plants are reasonably tough so that they suffer little damage from the beetles.

WINTER USE

Lima beans are particularly adaptable for quick freezing. Commercial frozen limas are one of the best frozen products on the market. In fact, they are so good and keep so well that you will have to be very skillful to equal their quality. The big difficulty in freezing limas is, in fact, a simple one; they are hard to shell.

COOKING

Use the Mystery Chef Method:
    Wash the lima beans.
    Boil rapidly 2 quarts of water to cover the beans in a
        3-quart enamel pot.
    Add 1 teaspoon of baking soda and the lima beans.
    Cook for one minute uncovered; it is important to leave
        uncovered.
    If the water foams, skim off the foam and reduce the heat.
    Strain off water and return the beans to the pot.
    Have water boiling rapidly in another 3-quart pot, metal
        or enamel.

Add 3 teaspoons of salt to the boiling water.
Add this boiling salt water to the beans in the enamel pot.
Cook for 8 minutes uncovered for young beans.
After cooking, strain the beans and return to pot.
Add butter and salt.
The hotter they are served the better.

SUMMARY

1. *Use Fordhook 2 42.*
2. *Treat seed with captan.*
3. *Dust with Sevin.*
4. *Cook by the Mystery Chef Method.*

Onions

Candlewood vegetable rating   10

Varieties	For	No. rows	No. ft.	Seed required	Source
White Queen	Cooking	2	76	½ oz.	Vilmorin-Andrieux
Chives	Salads			12 plants	Harris
Japanese Bunching	Salads	1	38	½ oz.	Harris
Danvers Yellow Globe	Cooking	4	152	½ oz.	Hart
Shallots	Flavoring	4	152	3 lbs.	Gurney
Leeks Musselburgh	Soup	2	76	1 pkt.	Unwins
		13			

Seed treatment   None
Number of rows   13
Rows planted   1 ft. apart
Size of lot   13 × 38 ft. = 494 sq. ft.
For winter use   Store in dry, cool, dark place

		PLANTING SCHEDULE IN IPSWICH				
	No. rows	Start in green-house	Trans-plant to flats	Trans-plant to garden	Plant in garden	Mature
Japanese Bunching	⅖	Feb. 20	Mar. 10	May 1		June 1
Japanese Bunching	⅕				May 16	June 20
Japanese Bunching	⅕				June 5	July 15

	No. rows	Start in green-house	Trans-plant to flats	Trans-plant to garden	Plant in garden	Mature
Japanese Bunching	⅓				July 9	Aug. 20
White Queen	1	Feb. 20	Mar. 10	May 1		July 15
White Queen	1	Apr. 5	May 5	June 10		Aug. 15
Danvers Yellow Globe	4	Feb. 20	Mar. 10	May 1		July 15
Shallots (sets)	4				Apr. 10	Sept. 1
Leeks	2	Feb. 20	Mar. 10	May 1		July 15

For a vegetable that is usually rated low on quality, it does seem peculiar to grow six varieties, far more than we grow of any other vegetable. The reason is that each variety is grown for a specific purpose. We enjoy onions, but we seldom use them as a vegetable by themselves (except for creamed or glacéed onions); more often they are used as an accompaniment to another food, such as steak, salad, or for soup. As such they are delicious, but if you were given a choice between peas and onions or asparagus and onions, probably the onions would lose out, and that accounts for their lower rating. We do admit, however, that when onions glacé appeared or the fragrance of onion soup filled the dining room on a cold night, we were tempted to raise the rating.

VARIETIES

We have tried the following varieties with good results:

Varieties	Quality
White Queen	Good
Danvers Yellow Globe	Good
Japanese Bunching	Good
Shallots	Good
Leeks Musselburgh	Good

Others tried:

Barletta	Red Globe	White Barcelona
Crystal	Red Southport	White Bunching
Hardy Bunching	Selected Ailsa Craig	White Leviathan
Prize Taker	Sweet Spanish	White Portugal
Prosperity Bunching	Tree Onions	Yellow Onion Sets

Each kind of onion we use, and the reason for its use, are described as follows:

Chives. Chives are bought in plant form. A dozen plants are enough, if they are planted in a place free of shade. We use chives in salads and sandwiches. Cream cheese and chives are always delightful. A few plants in the greenhouse or near a sunny window will supply a considerable amount all winter.

Japanese Bunching. We grow this onion only for the taste and fragrance it gives to salads. Whether this is sufficient reason, you will have to judge for yourself; at least it is an alternative to garlic.

We have 1 row for the bunching onions, planting $\frac{2}{5}$ of the row at the first planting and $\frac{1}{5}$ of the row at the other three planting dates. The first planting is 15 feet long. Because the seedlings must be 3 inches apart, 60 are required. The seeds are started on February 20 in a flat. About March 10, when the seedlings are 3 inches high, they are transplanted into two flats, with the seedlings $1\frac{1}{2}$ inches apart. On May 1, the seedlings, about 5 inches high, are set out in the garden. They mature about June 1 and last until around July 15, when they become too large and coarse to use. To prolong the season, and to have a continuity of young scallions, the seeds are planted directly in the garden (May 16, June 5, July 9); $\frac{1}{5}$ of a row is planted each time. In this way, they will last until September 1. It is pleasant to pick a young scallion and eat it while walking through the garden. It tastes so good that you may be tempted to eat two; then, very suddenly, you will find that one was plenty and two are far too many.

White Queen. This onion is bought in seed form. We plant two rows, or 76 feet, with the seedlings 4 inches apart, which requires 228 seedlings. The seeds are sowed in a flat in the greenhouse on February 20. When the seedlings are 2½ inches high, about March 10, they are transplanted into two flats, each containing about 60 plants, with the seedlings about 1½ inches apart. On May 1, when the seedlings are about 6 inches tall, they are transplanted in the garden. Another lot for the second row is started in the greenhouse on April 5, transplanted on May 5, and set out in the garden on June 10.

This onion is a small, white variety, about 2 inches in diameter when mature, of excellent appearance and quality. Picking should start as soon as it reaches a size of 1 inch in diameter, about July 15. This sounds all right on paper, but if you are interested in your plants, it may seem like sacrilege in the garden. To pick 36 onions, enough for 6 people, you have to use up 12 feet of row. However, that is what they are for and they should be used at their best (when they are small). This variety is particularly good for creamed or glacéed onions. When glacéed, they are delicious and deserve a very high vegetable rating. White Queen is certainly worth growing, but no more should be grown than can be used up before September 1. After that date, they grow large, and their quality full grown is not as good as Danvers Yellow Globe, at least in our garden.

Danvers Yellow Globe. This onion is bought in seed form. We plant 4 rows, or 152 feet, with the seedlings 6 inches apart. This requires 304 seedlings, for which ½ ounce of seed is needed. The seeds are started in the greenhouse on February 20. When the seedlings are 2½ inches tall (about March 10), they are transplanted into flats about 1½ inches apart. This requires six flats. On May 1, when the seedlings are 5 to 6 inches tall, they are transplanted in the garden. They are big enough to use in July, but we do not use them until we stop using White Queen, about September 1.

This is the best main crop onion we have tried from every point of view — quality, appearance, and freedom from trouble. We have never had any trouble with this variety except, very occasionally, a few cutworms. The appearance of the growing onions is most attractive. All in all, this is a most satisfactory vegetable to grow. Every seedling planted makes one good plant, which is more than you can say about many vegetables. These onions keep well in storage, last until about February 1, and are large and handsome. Their yield is good; 4 rows will produce 152 pounds, which is at a rate of 100 pounds to 100 feet (an average yield).

Shallots. These are a little-used vegetable, but they are of inestimable value. Few seed houses carry them. They have a very delicate flavor, and can be used where onions are too strong. Excellent for salads, they are also particularly good with scrambled eggs (country style) and with mushrooms. To cut them up into fine pieces, use an onion chopper, which can be bought in department stores or hardware stores.

This onion is bought in set form. We plant 4 rows, or 152 feet, with the bulbs planted 6 inches apart. This requires 304 bulbs, or 3 pounds of sets. They mature about September 1, and are then harvested and stored. Since they keep well, we have them for use until the new onions are mature the following spring. We grow more than we can use, for we find them welcome gifts. They will keep until June 15 the year after planting.

Leeks. We grow these onions, which are actually large scallions, only for vichyssoise; for that purpose alone they are worth growing. A leek is an onion with a long, thick stem that does not form a true bulb.

This onion, too, is bought in seed form. We plant 2 rows, or 76 feet, with the seedlings planted 6 inches apart. This requires 152 seedlings, for which we plant 2 packets of seed. The Musselburgh variety has proved most satisfactory at Candlewood.

The seed is started on February 20 and requires one flat. When the seedlings are 3 inches high, about March 10, they are transplanted into three flats with the seedlings 1½ inches apart. On May 1, the seedlings, about 5 inches high, are transplanted into the garden. They mature about July 15, and, when left in the ground, will last only until January 1.

PROCEDURE

To kill cutworms, the ground in which the onions are to be planted is sprayed twice, on April 13 and again on May 5, with Diazinon. This completely obviates cutworm trouble.

When the onion plants are about 6 inches high, we place mulch, 2 to 4 inches thick, of salt-marsh straw over the onion area. For this mulch, we use the remnants of what was used in the bean, corn, and pea area of the previous year. We find that the remnants are broken down into smaller pieces and are easier to handle in rows planted close together than is fresh straw. If salt-marsh straw is not available, salt-marsh hay or peat moss can be used; both are satisfactory. The few weeds that grow are easily pulled and the bed looks neat all summer. Our experience has been that our troubles, at least so far as onions are concerned, are over for the season. Nothing is left to do except to pick them.

WINTER USE

Either braid them together and hang them from a hook, or place them in onion bags and hang them. Since onions need good ventilation, store them in a cool, dry, dark, frost-proof place.

COOKING

We think there should be a slight flavor of onion in every salad. A Japanese bunching onion not over ¼ inch in diameter or over 4 inches long is excellent when cut into small pieces and mixed with the lettuce. It is mild and sweet and is the nicest of all onions to add to a salad; but if it is over ½ inch in diameter, it is too strong.

Its season is from June 1 to September 1; after September 1, shallots are very satisfactory. Chives can be added to any salad as a welcome addition for flavor. Garlic, a member of the onion family, is often used; if, however, you have ever bitten into a piece of garlic that somebody, by chance or call it what you will, has left in the salad, you will be cured of the garlic tradition at the very first bite.

Braised Onions (Onions Glacé)

Only small onions should be used; the White Queen is particularly well suited. For four people:

1 pint small onions	Few grains pepper
1 can consommé	3 tablespoons sugar
½ teaspoon salt	2 tablespoons butter

Put the onions into a small skillet with enough hot consommé to cover the bottom ½-inch in depth. Cover and cook quickly until one-half of liquid has been absorbed. Then turn the heat as low as possible. Add salt, pepper, sugar, and butter in bits. Cover and cook slowly, occasionally turning the onions until the liquid becomes glazed.

Creamed Onions

This is not food for summer, but on a cold winter's night it is hard to find anything more heartening, nourishing, and delicious.

For four people: peel and slice 6 large onions. Sauté in 4 tablespoons of butter and season with salt and pepper. Place the onions in a shallow Pyrex baking dish and keep warm while you make a cream sauce: melt 2 tablespoons of butter in a saucepan over low heat. Add and stir well 2 tablespoons of flour. Cook slowly and stir for 5 minutes. Add 1 cup of cream and 1 cup of milk. When mixture thickens, add 2 tablespoons of grated cheese and ½ teaspoon salt. Stir and cook until the sauce becomes creamy. The moment it becomes creamy, add it to the onions and sprinkle the top with bread crumbs, grated cheese, and paprika. Bake the onions in moderate oven 375° until the crumbs are brown.

Crème Vichyssoise

For this soup we grow leeks. We use them only for this soup, and they are excellent.

For four people:

> 2 large leeks or 8 small young ones
> 1 large onion or 2 small young ones
> 1 medium potato

Chop all together and put in a kettle. Add very little water, just enough so that it comes about halfway to the top of the vegetables. Cook until leeks are soft, and put through a blender. Put in a double boiler, and add the following:

> 1 pint chicken stock, or 1 can consommé
>   and 1 can water
> · 1 pint milk
> Salt
> Pepper
> A pat of butter

Heat and add ½ cup of cream.
Stir and heat until hot. Sprinkle with chopped chives.
In summer, place in refrigerator and serve very cold.

Onion Soup

Slice 12 medium-sized onions and put in skillet with 3 tablespoons butter. Cover and heat 25 minutes, stirring occasionally. Uncover, increase heat, add 1 tablespoon butter, and cook until brown.
Add 1 teaspoon Kitchen Bouquet.
Add 1 teaspoon flour.

Add pepper and salt.

Heat 2 cans of consommé and 1 can of water in a separate pot.

Put part of this in a blender and add one-half of onions. Run 1 minute.

Put shredded onions and consommé in pot and add balance of consommé.

Bring to a boil and cook for 15 minutes. This will extract the onion flavor and change the texture of the cooked onions so that they can be strained.

After straining, add the other half of the onions.

Simmer 5 minutes and serve.

Serve with croutons and grated Parmesan cheese.

For croutons, cut 4 slices bread into ½-inch pieces.

Put in skillet with 1 tablespoon butter.

Stir.

When bread is heated, add salt and grated cheese.

Keep warm in oven until wanted.

SUMMARY

1. *Plant many varieties.*
2. *For main crop, start seeds in greenhouse.*
3. *Use a mulch in the onion bed.*

Parsnips

Candlewood vegetable rating 20

        Variety: All American   *Source:* Harris

Seed treatment	Captan
Rows planted	3 ft. apart
Number of rows	1
Size of plot	3 × 38 ft. = 114 sq. ft.
Seed required for 150 ft. of row	1 oz.
For winter use	Protect and leave in ground

PLANTING SCHEDULE IN IPSWICH		
Sow	*Begin*	*Finish*
April 1	After first frost about Oct. 15	May 1

Most people do not like parsnips as they are usually cooked. But they can be so cooked that they may be enjoyed twice a week all winter. They take the place of potatoes and taste better.

VARIETIES

We have tried the following varieties with good results:

Varieties	*Quality*
All American	Good
Long Smooth White	Good
Hollow Crown	Good
Harris Model	Good

DIFFICULTIES

Our great difficulty was that all the seeds did not germinate. There often were empty spaces 2 feet long in the row. This meant that these spaces had to be replanted, which caused very uneven-looking rows. This condition is overcome by using the All American variety and treating the seeds with captan.

PROCEDURE

Parsnips, like most root crops, do not grow well in a tight, compact soil. Under such conditions, instead of growing one straight root, they divide into three or four, which make the root worthless. They must have a loose soil. The land where the parsnip row is to be set should be carefully spaded in the fall, and garden compost or manure well mixed in.

In the fall, the soil should be tested for acidity, and enough ground limestone added to bring the soil to pH 6.5. About April 1, plant the seeds in a V-shaped trench 2 inches wide at the top and ½ inch deep. After planting, the seeds should be covered, firmed down, and the row sprinkled with water. As the plants grow, thin them to 4 inches apart. This is important; otherwise, the roots crowd one another and develop poor form.

Parsnips should not be used until after the first heavy frost; only then do they attain their highest quality. It is often said that they are still better after being in the ground all winter; however, we believe they are best in November and December. They are still of good quality until the first of May.

WINTER USE

Parsnips can be left in the ground all winter. If they are protected with straw and a waterproof cover, like corrugated sheet steel, they can be dug easily even in the middle of winter with a heavy fall of snow on the ground. This makes them a very useful crop. We have found that parsnips keep better if left in the garden than if stored in a root cellar. It may be that something was wrong with our root cellar and that they would keep as well in a good one. In any case, that was our experience.

Of all the things grown in our garden, parsnips are about the easiest vegetable: they give good yields of high quality, with no pest trouble, and store well. Of what other vegetable can this be said?

COOKING

Cook parsnips exactly as you would cook julienne potatoes. They are sweet and crisp, with a flavor like sweet potatoes, and are delightful to eat.

Strange as it may seem, parsnip cream soup with chopped parsley floating on top is delicious. To make 1 pint of soup, enough for three people, cut up and boil 3 medium-sized parsnips and ½ medium-sized onion with enough water to cover until tender. It takes about 10 minutes. Then cool.

Put parsnips and onion and the water in which they are boiled into a blender. Add 1 cup of milk and run until the vegetables are thoroughly broken up; this requires about 5 minutes. Add 1 cup of cream, season with salt and pepper, and run for 1 minute more. Put in a double boiler and warm. Add chives and parsley when serving.

SUMMARY

1. *Use All American variety.*
2. *Treat seeds with captan.*
3. *For winter use, leave roots in garden; cover them with straw and sheet of corrugated steel.*

Peas

Candlewood vegetable rating   95

Varieties	No. rows	No. ft.	Seed required	Source
Alaska (coldframe)	2	76	2½ lbs.	Burpee
World's Record (Early)	1	38	1½ lbs.	Hart
Victory Freezer (Main)	4	152	5 lbs.	Unwins
Lincoln (Late)	4	152	5 lbs.	Harris
	11			

Seed treatment   Captan
Number of rows: Coldframe   2
Garden   9
Rows planted   3 ft. apart
Size of plot: Coldframe   6 × 38 ft. = 228 sq. ft.
Garden   27 × 38 ft. = 1026 sq. ft.
For winter use   Freeze — Results excellent

PLANTING SCHEDULE IN IPSWICH

Sowing dates	Variety		Begin	Finish	Days	Comparative quality
Mar. 18	Alaska	Coldframe	June 6	June 15	80	100
Mar. 29	World's Record	Garden	June 17	June 24	80	120
Mar. 29	Victory Freezer	Garden	June 26	July 3	89	120
Mar. 29	Victory Freezer	Garden	June 26	July 3	89	120
Mar. 29	Victory Freezer	Garden	June 26	July 3	89	120
Mar. 29	Victory Freezer	Garden	June 26	July 3	89	120
Apr. 21	Lincoln	Garden	July 1	July 5	71	140
May 6	Lincoln	Garden	July 6	July 11	67	140
May 14	Lincoln	Garden	July 12	July 17	58	130
May 18	Lincoln	Garden	July 18	July 24	60	120

*

There is only one way, in our opinion, to achieve the maximum table quality in fresh peas: grow them in your own garden. You cannot expect to find it in the peas you buy. Usually they are not the best sorts, they are picked when too old, and they are sold many hours after being picked. But the finest varieties, carefully grown, picked at the right stage, and eaten soon after picking — well, could anything be more delectable?

Topnotch, fresh peas are prime favorites of ours. During their necessarily short season, we have them every day. In reading articles about peas, you often see the statement that this plant is not recommended for the home garden because it takes up too much room. Nevertheless, to us, a garden without peas is ridiculous; it is like a nice house without a living room. When grown as they generally are, with one pound of seed to 100 feet of row, peas do take up a great deal of space. They are usually grown on brush, which has to be cut and carefully placed in the rows, and this entails time and considerable bother. But peas can be grown in such a manner as to produce a large quantity with a minimum amount of work.

VARIETIES

We have also tried the following varieties:

Admiral Beatty	Greater Progress	Early Bird
Alderman	Green Bayou	Early Delicious
Bunyards Latest	Heroine	Everbearing
Century of Progress	Hundred Fold	Foremost
Champion of England	Improved Telephone	Freezonian
Cordon Bleu	Latest of All	Miracle
De Clamest	Little Marvel	Napoleon
Frosty	Main Crop	No. 40
Giant Stride	Melting Sugar	Pedigree
Gilbo	Dwarf Champion	Phenomenon
Gladstone	Dwarf Gray Sugar	Potluck
Gradus	Dwarf Telephone	Prolific

Rondo	Stratagem	V.C.
Shasta	Stratagem Improved	Wando
Sparkle	Suttons Excelsior	Yukon

Included in this list are the peas with edible pods, or "sugar" peas, which, to us, are not worth eating.

Over the years we have tried out 47 different varieties and have finally settled down to these four as being the very best, all things considered: Alaska, World's Record, Victory Freezer, and Lincoln.

Alaska is a smooth-seeded pea, very small, and used extensively for canning. Because it is small, it is something of a chore to shell. However, its quality is good and it matures the earliest of all the peas that we have tried. Unquestionably, it is attractive and everyone exclaims "How wonderful"; but actually its quality is not as good as that of those that follow. Since peas are one of the earliest vegetables grown in the garden, it is always an event when they first arrive. The yield of Alaska in the coldframe is not high; nevertheless, there is enough to make it worthwhile. Another more important characteristic of this pea is that it germinates very well in a coldframe. Many of the smooth-seeded, early peas that we have tried in the coldrame were difficult to germinate.

World's Record is used for the earliest pea in the open garden. It is planted on March 29 and, on the average over the years, it matures on June 17. Immediately one asks: why not use Alaska? It would mature about four days earlier. However if Alaska is planted under the same conditions as World's Record, we find that World's Record yields more, is better in quality, and has a longer bearing season for each row.

World's Record has grown to a height of almost 48 inches at Candlewood. The pods, about 3 inches long, are a little smaller than the average. Yet it gives excellent crops of top quality. This variety has yielded an average of 25 quarts per 38-foot row over a period of several years.

For the next 4 rows, we use Victory Freezer, planted on March 29, the same date as the others, and maturing on July 3. Three of the rows are used for freezing. Victory Freezer is an excellent pea of very high quality.

The last 4 rows are planted with Lincoln, the highest quality of all the peas we have tried, and the one that withstands heat the best of all.

DATES

We have a pea season lasting from June 6 to July 24. Without the use of a coldframe and the modern peas, our season would be from June 21 until July 10, which is very short. March 29 is the earliest planting date advisable in Ipswich. We used to try to plant earlier, but found there was no advantage. March 18 in the coldframe and March 29 for outdoor planting may seem early for this part of the world, but, as a matter of fact, peas are pretty tough. They can even be planted in the fall just before the ground freezes, without their yield being hurt. You won't, however, get them to produce any earlier in the spring by so doing. The date on which you can make your first planting depends on the following factors: kind of soil, water level, weather, and the amount of rain. You cannot make early plantings on wet clay soil. The best conditions for early crops are a well-drained, sandy soil, sloping to the east, with a normal rainfall and an early spring. In Ipswich, the peas of the first row in the garden are ripe fifteen days after one half of the plants of that row are in bloom.

We have tried every suggestion offered by the experts to grow late peas, but we have come to the sad conclusion that our garden just will not produce them. As a matter of interest, the following experiments were tried; all were to no avail.

1. Plant peas deep and cover slowly as they grow.
2. Shade the rows.
3. Place wood slats over rows.
4. Use extra moisture.
5. Use Stimugerm.

6. Use gypsum mixed in the soil.

7. Have a water trough kept filled with water.

8. Do not tie up the peas, but let them grow on the ground. (This helps a little.)

Whether or not you can grow late peas probably depends solely on the ground in your garden. A cold clay soil with plenty of water seems to be needed. As far as we can make out, if you have early peas, you won't get late ones, and if you can raise late peas, you can't have early ones. So, all in all, you had better recognize what you have in the way of growing conditions and let it go at that!

We have noticed several facts about growing peas that seem unusual, to say the least. Peas of any given variety, when planted at the same time and under identical conditions, will vary as follows:

First, when planted on a slope toward the east they will mature earlier than those planted on the level.

Second, the late plantings on the slope do not mature; they turn yellow and die, although later plantings on the level do very well.

Third, when planted on the level, the quality of the peas was far better.

Fourth, when planted on the level, the yield is far higher. It is believed that this is all due to the fact that on an eastern slope the rays of the sun have a better chance to heat the ground and damage the roots.

DIFFICULTIES

Our greatest difficulty in the past was that, occasionally, a large part of a row, or even a whole row, would germinate very badly; there were bare spots in the row. This was particularly true of the 2 rows grown in the coldframe. This can be overcome in the garden by treating the pea seed with captan.

When the peas grow as they should, and the vines are numerous and heavy and the pods plentiful, the weight of the mass is hard to support. We had difficulty in putting in enough strong brush that would not break down. This trouble was overcome when we used pipes and chicken wire.

PROCEDURE

The 11 pea rows are spaced 3 feet apart. For each row of peas, we dig a trench 7 inches wide and, because our soil is light, 3 inches deep.

After the trench is dug, we scatter a handful of fertilizer (5–10–10) to every 7 feet of trench, and scuff it in with a four-pronged cultivator. Then we place 1-inch pipe, 6 feet long, at each end of the trench and every 8 feet in between. The pipes are 2 feet in the soil and 4 feet above, and are used to support the chicken wire to which we tie the pea vines. As a result, a solid support for the peas is provided even in high winds.

The soil should be quite damp when the peas are planted. In dry soil they do not germinate well, and a large percentage of seeds is lost. Our experiments with wetting the soil before planting have shown that dry soil is at least one cause for poor germination. So before planting, whether in the garden or in the coldframe (for an extra-early crop, if you have the space), soak the soil well by sprinkling. While the peas are growing, keep the rows well watered to produce a large crop. Treating the seed with captan will help, even if the soil is not as wet as it should be. Unless the soil is damp, however, even treated seeds will not do well.

The combination of soaking the soil and treating the seed is a happy one. In the past, we often had big patches in the pea rows where few or, sometimes, no seeds even came up. The use of captan and water put an end to that. We tried some inoculating experiments, but our results showed that the process did not help us in any way.

By the foregoing procedures, we can plant the pea seeds very thickly, far more thickly than is generally recommended. We use two and a half pounds of seeds for each 100 feet. This gives about fifty pea seeds to each foot of trench instead of the twelve to sixteen often used.

When the seeds are planted so closely, some of the vines either die or do not grow very tall. The percentage of such loss is much higher than with the usual method of planting. The cost of the seeds, however, is very little. What we are after is to produce as large a crop as possible in a small area. In any event, the cost of the extra amount of seed is less than the cost of preparing, seeding, and general cultural practice in an area twice as large. The seeds are broadcast in the trench as evenly as possible, and the trench is then filled in with soil.

Chicken wire 48 inches high is then attached to the poles. Our tasks are now over until the plants are high enough to tie to the wire. As soon as the peas are harvested, unfasten the wire, roll it up, and put it away for next year.

When the vines are about 12 inches high, tie them to the wire with soft twine. Start at one end of the row and tie the string to the end pipe. Then walk along the row and, about every 4 feet,

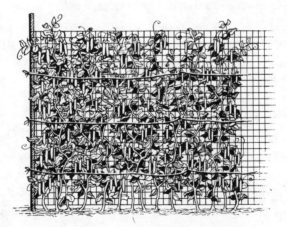

loop the string to the wire, pull tight and tie. These long loops will hold the vines in place until they take hold of the wire. As the peas grow, make similar loops for every foot of growth. It is easier to do this than to use brush; the pipes and wire will last for years.

When the peas come to the blossoming stage, they are a lovely sight of which you can well be proud. As the pods mature, it is interesting to see how thick they are and how easy to pick. The moment the pods in each row mature, the vines turn yellow and become very unsightly. They should be disposed of at once.

WINTER USE

Next to asparagus and lima beans, peas are, without question, the best vegetable to put in the freezer. Good ones properly prepared will last two years and have about 80 percent of the original quality. Of course, one of the great advantages of frozen peas is the ease with which they can be cooked; most of the work is done when they are frozen. To cook frozen peas, take them directly from the deep freeze and place them in hot water for 2 minutes. This will thaw them and bring them to room temperature for cooking.

COOKING

Use the Mystery Chef Method:

Boil rapidly 2 quarts of water in a 3-quart enamel pot.

Add 1 teaspoon of baking soda and the peas.

Cook for 1 minute uncovered; it is important to leave uncovered.

If water foams, skim off the foam and reduce heat.

Strain off water and return peas to pot.

Have water boiling rapidly in another 3-quart pot, metal or enamel.

Add 3 tablespoons of salt to boiling water.

Add this boiling salt water to the peas in the enamel pot.

Cook for 3 to 5 minutes, uncovered, depending on size.

After cooking, strain the peas, and return to pot.
Add butter and salt.

SUMMARY

1. Use Alaska, World's Record, Victory Freezer, and Lincoln.
2. Make many plantings.
3. Plant closely.
4. Support vines on chicken wire.
5. Use Mystery Chef Method for cooking.

Potatoes
(New)

Candlewood vegetable rating	80
Variety: Irish Cobbler	*Source:* Agway
Number of plantings	2
Number of rows planted	2
Rows planted	2 ft. apart
Size of plot	4 × 38 ft. = 152 sq. ft.
In the row 45 plants	10 in. apart
Seed potatoes required for this planting of 76 ft.	14 lbs.
Season	June 20–Aug. 1

PLANTING SCHEDULE IN IPSWICH

Plant	Mature	Finish
May 1	June 20	July 12
May 18	July 12	Aug. 1

What is better to eat than baby potatoes? Baby Irish Cobbler potatoes have something about them that is different from any young variety of vegetable. They are earthy and have a texture unlike anything else. Then, too, they have a kind of fragrance of the garden, and they make you think of all the lovely things that grow. Unless you have actually eaten these little potatoes, you can't imagine what they are like. Most people won't bother with them, and they do not realize what they miss!

Of course, all efficient gardeners will throw up their hands in horror at the idea of picking such little potatoes. If you doubt this statement, just ask one to do it. In the past, of all the things that good gardeners were asked to do by their crazy employers, none caused more anguish than being asked to pick potatoes, beets, and carrots before they were full grown. But what is the use of having available such delicacies, if you don't use them. They are truly in the luxury class; they should be grown and used as such. Plan to use them up by August 1, for their quality diminishes after that date.

VARIETIES

We have tried the following varieties for baby potatoes to be eaten when under 1½ inches in diameter:

Variety	Quality
Irish Cobbler	Excellent
Green Mountain	Fair
Katahdin	Fair

It is interesting to note that, although Irish Cobbler is the best for the baby potatoes, it ranks as only fair for storage. On September 1, the Irish Cobblers, although fairly large, were still better than the small Katahdins, but in fall and winter, their quality diminishes. If you will consult the Candlewood Rating Table in "Vegetables of Quality," Part One, you will notice that baby potatoes are rated 80 (high in the scale), and winter potatoes are rated only 10.

YIELDS

It is almost ridiculous to speak of yields as far as baby potatoes are concerned. If you are willing to pick these potatoes when they are about one-quarter grown, just for the pleasure of eating them, the yield is so small, it shouldn't even be considered. From a 38-foot row, we obtain about 100 baby potatoes 1 to 1½ inches in diameter. Generally, we dig 5 baby potatoes for each person.

DIFFICULTIES

The gaily colored yellow and black potato bugs used to present a great difficulty, but that problem now is easily overcome if the plants are sprayed with Sevin on a regular schedule.

PROCEDURE

Some time before the first of May, we dig a shallow trench about 3 inches deep and 12 inches wide, where the potatoes are to be planted, and spread in the trench a layer about 1 to 2 inches thick of garden compost. This is dug into the top 3 inches of the trench and mixed well with the soil. The seed potatoes are planted on May 1 and May 18. Ordinarily the seed potatoes arrive at our local cooperative store during the last few days of April. If they are not planted within a few days, they will start to sprout. We found that we could keep them from sprouting by storing them in the refrigerator. Since only one-half of those we buy (or about seven pounds) have to be stored, that is not too much of a problem. The great advantage of doing this is that the season for the baby potatoes can be extended about one month, and if you acquire a fondness for these delicacies, you will not mind the minor inconvenience.

The seed potatoes, which you will have to obtain locally, should be cut into 3 or 4 pieces, and you must make certain that each piece has at least one eye. Seed potatoes are identical to those you can obtain in the supermarket, except that they have been certified as free of disease.

As soon as the plants are a few inches above ground, we spread a 4-inch layer of salt-marsh straw. If it is not available, we use salt-marsh hay. The combination of the spray and the straw does wonders for the potatoes.

It is a little difficult to know just when to pick the baby potatoes. You can tell only by digging around the plants about the time the flower buds show. It is necessary to try a few plants several feet apart, since they do not all mature at the same time. Start using them when they are about 1 inch in diameter. It is unfortunate if you happen to uncover one large plant first and dig up a quantity too small to use, or if you happen to find a little plant first and then wait too long before starting to pick. The only safe way is to try several plants before you dig any. Baby potatoes do not keep well, and should not be stored.

COOKING

We boil and serve the baby potatoes with their skins on. This method of cooking seems to retain the flavor. When they are cut on your own plate, spread with plenty of butter, and sprinkled with a small amount of chopped parsley, they are really delicious. Another way to cook baby potatoes is to bake them and then eat them, skins and all. Since they shrink tremendously in baking, medium-sized ones should be used for this purpose.

Potatoes
(For Fall and Winter)

Candlewood vegetable rating   10

Variety: Green Mountain   *Source:* Agway

Number of plantings	1
Number of rows planted	2
Rows planted	2 ft. apart
Size of plot	4 × 38 ft. = 152 sq. ft.
In the row 45 plants	10 in. apart
Seed potatoes required for this planting of 152 ft.	14 lbs.
Season	Aug. 15–Apr. 1

PLANTING SCHEDULE IN IPSWICH		
Plant	*Mature*	*Finish*
May 1	Sept. 1	Sept. 15

While potatoes are a necessity, and on occasions when you are cold and hungry nothing takes their place, nevertheless, they are only 10 on the Candlewood Rating Table. This rating you may accept or not, depending on your hunger and temperament.

VARIETIES

We have tried the following varieties:

Variety	*Quality*
Green Mountain	Excellent
Katahdin	Excellent
Chippewa	Good
Northern Gold	Good
Irish Cobbler	Fair

Red Bliss	Fair
Suttons Snowball	Fair

As far as our choice goes, we pick Irish Cobbler for baby potatoes and Green Mountain for fall and winter use. Green Mountain is an excellent variety, of good size and large yield, and it keeps well. We use these potatoes about three times a week, which is a low consumption for potatoes by most standards.

The yield of Green Mountain potatoes grown on garden compost, mulched with salt-marsh straw, and sprayed with Sevin is really enormous. In 1950 at Candlewood, we dug one-half of a row, 19 feet, at one time just to weigh the potatoes and determine the exact yield. From this half row, which was representative of the whole, we obtained forty-five pounds of potatoes, all of excellent size and quality. This is at the rate of 240 pounds per 100 feet of row.

DIFFICULTIES

Same as for New Potatoes.

PROCEDURE

Same as for New Potatoes.

WINTER USE

Store in a moist, cool cellar, about 36 to 40 degrees, with good air circulation.

Radishes

Variety: Champion	*Source:* Harris
Seed treatment	None
Number of plantings	14
Number of rows planted	2
Rows planted	1 ft. apart
Size of plot: Hotframe	1½ × 5½ ft. = 8 sq. ft.
Garden	2 × 38 ft. = 76 sq. ft.
In the row	½ in. apart
Seed required	2 oz.
Season	May 18 to frost, about Oct. 10

PLANTING SCHEDULE IN IPSWICH

	Plant	Mature	Finish
Hotframe	Apr. 1	May 5	May 20
Garden	Apr. 15	May 18	Sept. 30

After April 15, we plant ⅕ of a row, or 8 feet, every ten days, up to September 1.

*

Certainly the radish is an unimportant little vegetable; nevertheless, a few, once in a while, are very nice. They are good with cocktails and in a salad. They are also ego builders because they are exceedingly easy to grow, and are one of the first vegetables to mature. For this reason alone they should be grown, even if you are not fond of them.

DIFFICULTIES

At planting time, the furrow should be sprayed with Diazinon to ward off the cabbage root maggot. Our experience at Craigston

has been that the more mature the radish, the most susceptible it is
to the devastating effects of this insect.

PROCEDURE

Sow 8 feet in the row at each planting. A continuous supply of
radishes and bunching onions is needed for salads, so it is a good
idea to plant these two vegetables alongside the lettuce. Thinning
is essential if you are to avoid all top-growth and no radishes.

Rhubarb

Variety: Valentine   Source: Burpee

Number of rows   ½
Rows planted   5 ft. apart
Size of plot   5 × 19 ft. = 95 sq. ft.
In the row 6 plants   3 ft. apart
Season   May 4–Aug. 20
For winter use   Freeze — Results excellent

The stalks are a bright red, not only on the outside but all the way through. Sauces and pies made from it are a beautiful, rich crimson of fine flavor. Since Valentine does not go to seed, the stalks can be picked almost all summer, up to August 20. If you happen to like rhubarb pie, this is quite an advantage.

Rhubarb comes very early in the spring and is really the earliest of all things picked in the garden, except radishes and, of course, parsnips, which were grown and left in the ground over the winter. As one of the earliest crops, it is very welcome to the home gardener. Most gardens have far too many rhubarb plants, so much is wasted. Six plants will supply a tremendous amount of rhubarb.

VARIETIES

We have tried the following varieties:

Variety	Quality
Valentine	Excellent
Chipman's Canada Red	Good
Strawberry	Good

Others tried:

MacDonald   Ruby   Victoria

DIFFICULTIES

None.

PROCEDURE

Simply buy good roots and put them in the ground. Plant in October so that the crowns are barely visible on the surface. There will be very little to pick until one year from the following spring because rhubarb is a hardy perennial. You should consider planting it in a permanent location, perhaps near other perennials, such as the raspberries and asparagus.

The stalks should be pulled from the plant rather than cut, and may be harvested for three to four weeks the second season and up to eight weeks thereafter. The large seed stalks should be removed as soon as they are in evidence, and the leaves should be allowed to develop during the summer to provide strength to the crowns.

COOKING

Rhubarb, as it is generally cooked, is a watery, sour, and tasteless concoction not worth eating, but good rhubarb properly cooked is certainly delicious.

An excellent way of cooking rhubarb is to boil the cut-up stalks, in enough water to cover them, until they are thoroughly stewed. Then strain through a colander into a pot and boil the liquid until it becomes half its original volume. Add 1 cup of sugar, the grated rind of an orange and some lemon peel, and 4 more cups of rhubarb stalks cut in lengths about 1 inch long. Keep boiling until the newly added stalks are cooked; do not overcook. Cool, and you have a most delicious dessert. This is also a good filling for rhubarb pie.

WINTER USE

Cook as suggested and freeze in plastic cartons.

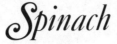Spinach

Candlewood vegetable rating 30
           Variety: America   *Source:* Burpee
             Seed treatment   Captan
             Number of rows 5
              Rows planted 1 ft. apart
                Size of plot 5 × 38 ft. = 190 sq. ft.
              Seed required ¼ lb.
          Season: Garden May 21–June 20

PLANTING SCHEDULE IN IPSWICH

	Plant	*Begin*	*Finish*
2 rows	Apr. 1	May 21	June 10
3 rows	Apr. 10	June 1	June 20

Spinach is a cool season vegetable that cannot tolerate the July and August heat. It develops best when grown as either a spring or fall crop, and will bolt to seed in midsummer. America, our favorite variety, is more resistant to bolting than most Savoy types (those with wrinkled leaves), although it matures several days later than other varieties (fifty days rather than forty days).

Spinach, as it is generally raised and cooked, is beyond the pale. Why anyone bothers to eat it is beyond comprehension. In many restaurants, it is served as a cold, watery mass with a piece of egg floating on it, and you might as well eat grass, for all the pleasure you find in eating such a concoction.

But good spinach is something else, particularly since it matures at a time when its only rivals are asparagus, lettuce, and parsnips. We enjoy it so much when it first comes in that we use it every other day. But spinach in summer is another matter. There are too many better vegetables, so we don't bother with it.

VARIETIES

We have tried the following varieties with good results:

Variety	Quality
America	Good
Bloomsdale Savoy	Good
New Zealand (not a true spinach)	Good
Viking	Good
Winter Bloomsdale	Good

Others tried:

King of Denmark	Prickley
Perpetual Spinach	Tampala

DIFFICULTIES

Poor germination of seed, which is cured by the use of captan, and cutworm trouble, which is cured by spraying the ground twice, on April 13 and again on May 5, with Diazinon, are the troubles we have encountered.

WINTER USE

It hardly seems worthwhile to us to process or freeze spinach, since it is not one of our favorite vegetables. Then, too, fresh spinach can be bought in the market all winter.

COOKING

Use the Mystery Chef Method:
    Wash the spinach well. To do this, put the spinach in a large pan of water, let it stand for a few minutes, and lift

the spinach out of the pan. This will allow the sand and dirt to stay in the pan. If the water is drained off the spinach, the dirt will remain with it.

Boil rapidly 2 quarts of water in a 3-quart enamel pot.

Add 1 teaspoon of baking soda and then the spinach.

Cook for 1 minute uncovered; it is important to leave uncovered.

If water foams, skim off the foam and reduce heat.

Strain off water and return spinach to pot.

Have water boiling rapidly in another 3-quart pot, metal or enamel.

Add 3 tablespoons of salt to boiling water.

Add this boiling salt water to the spinach in the enamel pot.

Cook for 8 minutes uncovered.

After cooking, strain the spinach and return to pot.

Add butter and salt.

Now if you want spinach that is really something extra, add to the spinach in the strainer:

> 1 teaspoon butter
> 2 tablespoons cream

Mash with a spoon and force the spinach through strainer into a saucepan.

Add $\frac{1}{4}$ teaspoon nutmeg and 1 teaspoon cheese.

Stir, cover, and simmer 5 minutes.

SUMMARY

1. Use America variety.
2. Use Mystery Chef Method.

Winter Squash

Candlewood vegetable rating 20

Variety: Golden Delicious *Source:* Harris

Seed treatment	Captan
Number of rows	½
Rows planted	6 ft. apart
Size of plot	12 × 19 ft. = 228 sq. ft.
In the row 4 hills	5 ft. apart
Seed required	2 pkts.
Yield from this bed of 20 ft. with 4 hills	150 lbs.
Yield of squash per 100 ft. of row	750 lbs.
Season	Oct. 10–Feb. 1
For winter use	Store in cool, dry place with good circulation of air

PLANTING SCHEDULE IN IPSWICH	
Plant	*Mature*
June 1	Oct. 10

*

There is a tremendous difference in the varieties of squash. Some are distinctly not worth eating, but the few varieties are really excellent.

VARIETIES

We have tried the following varieties of squash with good results:

Variety	*Quality*
Golden Delicious	Excellent

Buttercup	Good
Waltham Butternut	Good
Table Queen — Acorn	Good

Others tried:

Des Moines	Green Gold
Delicious	Golden Hubbard
Delecta	Blue Hubbard
Warren Turban	

With regard to the varieties, Golden Delicious, a large, golden orange squash, heads the list. The texture is slightly lighter, somewhat like a summer squash, and the taste very delicate and more delicious than Buttercup. It is beautiful to look at as it grows in the garden, and its lovely orange color stands out in a most striking fashion.

Buttercup is second. This is a small green squash about 6 to 8 inches in diameter and about 3 inches across. It looks like a ball that has been flattened. The texture, color, and taste are all perfect. It is a very good yielder, and is free, at least in our garden, of squash borers. All in all, it seems an excellent vegetable.

Butternut, a brown dumbbell-shaped squash, is third. The texture of this is like that of a sweet potato and a little on the dry side. The taste and color are good, but we have not found it the equal of Buttercup. It is not troubled by the squash borer and is an excellent yielder.

Table Queen has been exceptionally prolific at Craigston, and has been subject to neither disease nor pests. It stores well and is a welcome addition to a cold winter's night fare. We cut it in half, put 1 tablespoon butter and 1 tablespoon brown sugar in each cavity, and bake at 300° for about 1 hour.

Although the squash are large enough to eat in September, we never use them before the first frost. We find that, as long as there are corn, beans, and limas, we just do not eat squash. But at the first heavy frost, about October 10, these vegetables are finished in the garden; then we are glad to have squash and the other "after frost" vegetables. From October 10 on, we use squash once or twice a week until well into the new year.

DIFFICULTIES

Our only difficulty has been the squash borer. Some squash are much more vulnerable than others. Golden Delicious seems the squash most fancied by the squash borer. Des Moines, Buttercup, Acorn, and Butternut, when we grew them, were not touched by the squash borer.

PROCEDURE

A hole 15 inches in diameter and 3 inches deep should be scooped out where the hills are to be planted. A shovelful of garden compost should be worked into the hole and the soil returned. The seeds, ten to a hill, should be planted directly over the compost and the seedlings thinned to five. The plants grow very well on compost.

As we grow only four hills of squash, which takes up half a row, the other half of the row is used for growing four hills of cucumbers. Squash and cucumbers need plenty of room. The adjacent rows should be at least 6 feet away. The vines will often grow to a length of 20 feet; they should be moved, occasionally, so that they won't bother the neighboring rows, or extend through the fence to tempt the woodchucks.

The squash vine borer is the greatest menace that the plants have. Unless they are destroyed, the borers can ruin every vine. It is so disheartening to see the leaves curl up and shrivel. However, if you dust with a preparation like Ortho Tomato Vegetable Dust, which contains both methoxychlor and rotenone, every borer can be destroyed before it enters the vine, and what a satisfaction that is. Sevin is also effective.

The four hills used to produce about 100 pounds, but one year, grown on compost and sprayed, they produced 150 pounds. Another year, however, all calculations were upset. The four squash hills were in an area that had been used for celery the previous year. The celery had been grown in trenches 16 inches wide in which had been spread a layer of garden compost, 2 inches deep, that was worked into the trench. The squash was planted over the old trenches and, because of the combination of this exceedingly rich soil, spraying, and lots of rain, it produced as never before — almost 500 pounds, with one squash weighing forty pounds.

This brings up the interesting question on the frequency of the use of compost. Forty-pound squashes are not practical for a small household, nor could we use one-fifth of the squash produced that year. It would seem, so far as squash is concerned, that it would be better to grow it in soil enriched with compost only every other year.

WINTER USE

Store the squash in a dry cool place with good air circulation. They can be kept until about the first of February, with the loss of only a few.

See "Freezing and Storing," Part Three.

SUMMARY
1. Use Golden Delicious.
2. Spray to eliminate squash vine borer.

Strawberry, or Husk, Tomatoes

Variety: Strawberry Tomato

Seed treatment	None
Size of plot	6 × 19 ft. = 114 sq. ft.
Rows planted	3½ ft. apart
Number of rows	½
In the row 5 plants	4 ft. apart
Seed required	1 pkt.
Season	Sept. 15–Dec. 1
Storing	Pick Oct. 5 and store in a cool, dry place

PLANTING SCHEDULE IN IPSWICH

Start (in greenhouse)	Transplant to flats when 1 in. high	Transplant to garden	Mature	Finish
Mar. 15	about Apr. 2	June 12	Sept. 15	Oct. 10

Strawberry, or husk, tomatoes, a very low-rated garden product, are no necessity in any garden. Yet they are interesting to watch grow, and the fruit is delightful to eat with cocktails. It is called a tomato because it looks like one, but it belongs to a different genus, classified as *Physalis pubescens,* and originated in South America. When they are first set out in the garden, the little plants are about 6 inches high and about 3 inches in diameter. They are set 4 feet apart in the row. So much room is left available for them that they look rather lonely. However, they soon begin to grow, and about the end of August they suddenly leap forward. You can almost see them grow. By October 1, each plant measures 6 feet across.

The husks are about ¾ of an inch in diameter and the fruit inside is about ½ inch in diameter. When fully ripe, the tomato is yellow in color with solid flesh. They are very good if husked and served on ice with cocktails. If you don't like cocktails, then don't raise strawberry tomatoes.

In October, all the large and fully ripe fruit can be collected and stored. It will keep in good condition until the first of December.

DIFFICULTIES

None, except cutworms.

PROCEDURE

Start the seeds in the greenhouse about March 15 in a flat. When the seedlings are 1 inch high, about April 2, transplant fifteen to another flat. Although only five are needed in a 19-foot row, it is well to raise a few extra so that only the best are planted.

By September, there will be more than a hundred fruit on each plant. The husk will turn yellow and fall off when the fruit is fully ripe. Inside the husk is the tomato, green when not ripe, and yellow when fully mature. By the beginning of September, there will be a few ripe ones; by September 15, there will be plenty.

About October 5, just before the severe frost is due, pick all the

fruit in yellow husks that are on the ground or on the plants. Add to these all that mature up to the first frost. Store in a cool, dry place. If properly stored, these will last until December 1.

After the frost has come and the plants have been removed from the garden, it is well to rake up all of the strawberry tomatoes left on the ground; otherwise, they will seed themselves the following year and become a nuisance. For the same reason, it is better not to put the plants in the compost pile. One year, at the end of the fall, we happened to throw the old plants on the top of the compost. The next spring the compost pile was covered with hundreds of little strawberry tomato plants.

COOKING

Strawberry Tomato Jam

Put the juice of 1 lemon in a cup and fill it with water. Put it in a deep saucepan, and add 2 cups of sugar. Boil syrup 5 minutes. Husk the ripe tomatoes, cut in halves, and put 4 cups of the halved tomatoes into the pot. Boil for 1½ hours, put in glasses, and seal while hot. Makes a delicious jam.

SUMMARY

1. Good only with cocktails or for preserving.
2. Allow plenty of room between plants.

Tomatoes

Candlewood vegetable rating 30

Varieties: Moreton Hybrid
(16 plants)   *Source:* Harris
Red Cherry (3 plants) —
Small fruit   *Source:* Burpee
Seed treatment   None
Number of rows   1
Rows planted   3 ft. apart
Size of plot   3 × 38 ft. = 114 sq. ft.
In the row 19 plants   2 ft. apart
Seed required for each variety   1 pkt.
Season   July 20–Oct. 25

PLANTING SCHEDULE IN IPSWICH

Start in greenhouse	Transplant to flats when 1½ in. high	Put in pots	Transplant to garden	Mature	Finish
Mar. 15	About Mar. 26	Apr. 30	June 1	July 20	Oct. 10

In our opinion, tomatoes are an overrated vegetable, but many people think just the opposite. For salads there are many other vegetables that are better, and as for cooked vegetables, who would prefer stewed tomatoes to the really good vegetables? And what can be of less pleasure to eat than the stewed tomatoes at the ordinary restaurant? Tomatoes baked with a sprinkling of brown sugar are good, but the goodness is due largely to the sugar. Cold, sliced tomatoes, sprinkled with sugar, are pleasant on a hot day; yet would not anyone swap them for a good ear of corn?

VARIETIES

We have tried the following with good results:

Variety	Quality
Moreton Hybrid	Excellent
Waltham Scarlet (unavailable)	Excellent
Belmont	Good
Bonny Best	Good
Carter Sunrise	Good
Pennheart	Good
Red Cherry	Good
Rutgers	Good
Yellow Pears	Good

Others tried:

Best of All	Golden Jubilee	Red Cloud
Comet	Homestead Abundant	Red Pear
Crystal White	Jet Star	Saint Pierre
Current	Marglobe	Supersonic
Earliana	Paris Favorite	Tangerine
Fordhook Hybrid	Premier	Valiant
Giant Ponderosa	Pritchards Scarlet Topper	Victor

Of all the varieties tried, Waltham Scarlet was outstanding. Unfortunately, it is no longer available, unless you had the foresight to save the seeds. Today there are over 100 varieties available, and you will have to rely on your own trial-and-error methods to select the one best suited for your purposes, keeping in mind the qualities, such as size, color, maturity dates, yields, and so on, which you deem most important. Naturally, as with other vegetables, no one variety will offer all the best qualities, but try to come as close as you can to perfection. In Essex County, we have found Harris' Moreton Hybrid most satisfactory.

DIFFICULTIES

Ortho Tomato Vegetable Dust is effective in preventing most diseases and insect damage on tomato plants. It contains captan, methoxychlor, and rotenone.

PROCEDURE

About one week before setting the plants in the garden, dig holes about 18 inches in diameter and 4 inches deep where the plants are to grow. Put one spadeful of garden compost into each hole and mix well with the soil. The hole should then be filled with the soil that was dug out. If garden compost is not available, a trowelful of Bovung (dried cow manure) and a trowelful of bone meal can be used.

Before the plants are set, 7½-foot pipes, 1 inch in diameter, should be placed at the ends of the row with one in between. The pipes are to be driven 1½ feet into the soil and a wire strung along the top. Stick three bamboo poles about ¾ inch in diameter into the ground at each plant and tie to the wire. As the plants grow, only three stems are allowed to form; the others should be pinched off from time to time. The bamboo poles are about 6 inches apart, which gives plenty of room for us to tie the stems to the poles. This provides a strong support that will not fall over even in high winds. After the vines reach the top of the poles about September 1, we cut off the vine tips and extra foliage to allow the sunlight full access to the fruit. This will hasten the ripening of the last fruit. Before the October 10 frost, all the large and fully ripe fruit can be collected and stored. The green ones can be ripened by being laid in flats in the shed. They are not of as good quality as those picked ripe in the garden, but they are still pleasant to eat, and, saving them this way, you can extend the season until about the end of October.

YIELDS

We found that the yield could be increased tremendously and the quality improved by the use of garden compost and the three-stem system. This was particularly noticeable after the middle of September. On one plant grown without compost, the leaves started to come off and the fruit turned yellow. The yield of this plant was about three-quarters that of the plants grown on compost.

COOKING

A favorite recipe is broiled tomatoes. For each person two tomatoes are skinned, cut into pieces, and stewed with 2 tablespoons of sugar. No water is added. The tomatoes are crushed and cooked until tender. For each person, one large or two small tomatoes are sliced and covered with butter and brown sugar. These are broiled until the sugar has melted and been absorbed. The tomato stew is placed on toast and the broiled tomatoes on top. Our record to date is that all the plates are empty when removed.

Sliced tomatoes, very cold and sprinkled with granulated sugar, are very nice on a hot summer day. There is just enough acidity in the tomatoes to make the sugar welcome.

SUMMARY

1. *Use Moreton Hybrid.*
2. *Put garden compost under each plant.*
3. *Use three-stem method.*
4. *Support on poles.*
5. *Dust with Ortho Tomato Vegetable Dust.*

Part Three

Here is information about our methods of maintaining an attractive and productive vegetable garden.

The importance and methods of properly cooking the vegetables to produce the best taste are discussed.

We here describe our techniques for freezing vegetables in what we consider to be the quickest and most efficient method. Vegetables from the garden served in January are a mouth-watering delicacy.

Care of the Garden

WEEDING

One of life's less entertaining tasks is weeding. It is enough to deter some from having a vegetable garden at all. It is tedious and time-consuming, yet the task is absolutely essential if the maximum yield is to be obtained and if the garden is to be aesthetically pleasing. It will require determination and perseverance to forgo the tennis courts or golf course in favor of weeding; however, you might as well buy your vegetables in the market if this job is not faithfully done on a regular schedule. A garden should not only yield vegetables of the highest quality but also be a source of pleasure. We cannot see any justification for a garden that looks neglected and produces vegetables that clearly have lost out to weeds in the competition for moisture, nutrients, light, and space.

Weeding must be started well before the weeds are 1 inch tall. They are easily dispatched at this size with a hoe or cultivator, and if you are persistent, especially in the early summer, the task will not become monumental. Make a habit of taking your favorite weeding tool to the garden on each trip; every five minutes counts. When the vegetable seedlings are small, one has to be especially careful not to disturb the roots, and often hand weeding is necessary.

At Craigston, we have found the use of a small garden tractor ideal for keeping the area between the rows neat and free of weeds. This cuts the weeding workload in half, although it does mean wider spacing between rows and therefore a larger garden area. A discussion of the use of mulch comes later in this chapter.

THINNING

Plants need space in which to grow and develop so that they are not competing with each other for moisture and nutrients. By following the directions on the packet, you can space the seedlings properly when you first set them out in the garden; nevertheless, seeds often come up too thickly and must be thinned. Choose the weakest plants and be careful not to disturb the roots of those you intend to leave. It is best to do this when the soil is moist. It is difficult to destroy willfully the life of a young plant, but you must be resolute; just keep in mind that it is for the best. The plants you leave will be stronger and healthier and better producers. Sometimes the thinnings can be successfully transplanted if you choose strong seedlings and water them well for several days. For one who finds the thinning job particularly wrenching, transplanting helps take some of the sting out of it. The thinnings of some vegetables can be eaten — carrots, beets, and lettuce. These you will find are a real treat; they often taste better than those that are closer to maturity.

WATERING

A uniform water supply is essential for a successful vegetable garden. No watering at all is better than sporadic sprinkling. A great deal of damage can be done if you water faithfully and thoroughly for a few weeks, or if there is plenty of rain, and then you suddenly stop watering, or there's a dry spell. Plants become dependent on a constant water supply. This is one area where we feel buying top quality is important. Inexpensive, lightweight sprinklers tend to have a short life span. The sprinkler you use should throw a continuous shower of fine drops so that the water will not wash away seeds or the soil above them. Always water thoroughly; unless you soak the soil several inches deep, you might as well not bother to water at all. The ideal time to water is in the morning; next best is late afternoon. You will lose a lot of water through evaporation and will risk burning the plants if you try to water in the hot noonday sun.

MULCHING

Mulching can be an invaluable aid to gardening. The mulch does several things, all of which are most helpful.

1. It prevents the sun from baking the soil.
2. It keeps the temperature of the soil low, which reduces evaporation of the water in the soil.
3. It protects the soil and keeps it loose in texture (not compacted), so that it absorbs rainwater readily and loses less surface water.
4. It keeps weeds to a minimum.
5. It improves the quality of the vegetables.
6. It keeps vegetables clean and free from mud spattering.

When you use mulch, it is necessary to weed only once; put on the mulch, and there is very little weeding left to do. If you depend on rain for watering the garden, or if water is scarce for sprinkling, then the use of mulch is really a necessity. Various materials can be used, including the following:

Buckwheat hulls	Peat moss	Salt-marsh hay
Grass cuttings	Sawdust	Salt-marsh straw
Leaves	Straw	Black plastic mulch

We have found salt-marsh straw the best mulch for us, with salt-marsh hay a close second. Salt straw is the material that floats on the marshes and is left deposited on the edges by high tides and wind. After a storm and a high tide, it is easy to collect truckloads along the marsh edges. Salt hay can be bought at most local garden supply stores. Peat moss ranks third; it is more expensive and much harder to spread, but it gives the garden an excellent appearance and makes it look neat and orderly. Buckwheat hulls are good, but, again, they are hard to spread. Grass cuttings are likely to become messy and soggy with mildew. For a garden of any size, the black plastic mulch is totally impractical. It is difficult to lay and can only be used when one is mulching seedlings; we find it most unattractive in appearance, although it may be useful for a small planting.

The mulch should be applied after the ground has become warm and when the plants are about 4 inches high. If the mulch is put on before the ground is warm, the germination of the seeds will be delayed. Certain plants (potatoes) will grow through a mulch (except black plastic), but it seems better to wait until the plants are above the soil before you apply the mulch.

Salt straw or salt hay mulch is spread to a depth of 3 or 4 inches. During the summer, part of the mulch breaks up and becomes integrated with the soil, but most of it can be raked up in the fall and used again. It is better to use this straw, which has been exposed to the elements for one year, around beets, carrots, lettuce, and onions, since it is a little easier to handle in the close-growing rows than the fresh straw, which is stiff.

Any fine straw that is left should be raked up and put on the compost pile. Thus, most of the straw that is used eventually finds its way into the soil, either directly or through the compost pile.

PESTS

Pests — what an unpleasant word! It covers a multitude of sins: animals, insects, and diseases. Fortunately, at least to date, we have had few troubles; what we have had were easily controlled. This is not an article on all pests; it concerns only those that have bothered us.

Rabbits

Probably the worst potential source of trouble in our garden has been the rabbit problem. The woods around the garden are filled with them. They love asparagus, beans, lettuce, limas, and peas. Beans and peas, when about 1 inch high, seem to be their particular favorites. A whole row may be ruined overnight.

However, rabbits are easily controlled by a wire fence 26 inches above the ground. We use chicken wire of about ½-inch mesh, 3 feet high. We drive pipes along the border about 8 to 12 feet apart and fasten the wire to the pipes. The wire screen is buried 5 inches in the ground. A stiff wire screen is strong enough to be kept straight without sagging between the pipes. Often the rabbits will start to burrow under the wire, but 5 inches is enough to stop them.

Squirrels

Squirrels are partial to corn; the sweeter it is, the more they like it. If there is 1 row of extra sweet corn among the varieties planted, that row will be selected by the squirrels for their own. We tried an electric wire, activated by a storage battery and a high voltage transformer, similar to that used for cattle, on top of the wire screen. While it did some good, it did not stop the squirrels completely and was not successful. When the transformer was connected to the house current, the squirrels received an awful surprise as they stepped on the wire to get to the corn. It did not kill them, but it certainly left them terrified, and their eagerness for corn diminished.

We have some elm trees between the house and the garden at Candlewood. Over the years, every spring when the elm seeds emerged from the bud stage, many squirrels would come to eat them. They would generally be active between seven and eight o'clock in the morning. Sometimes so many would come that the lawn was littered with the tips of the branches they had eaten off. It is said that some people seize this opportunity to shoot the squirrels.

Woodchucks and raccoons

Other animals, particularly woodchucks and raccoons, are less easily foiled and are very destructive. One woodchuck can leave his teethmarks on almost every squash and pumpkin in the garden in only a few days. We had this experience at Craigston, and it was most disheartening. Fortunately, we were in the process of making grape jelly at the time and it occurred to us that, if paraffin preserves a jar of jelly, it may well save a scarred Hubbard squash from spoilage. We brushed hot paraffin on all the damaged areas and were delighted that they stored well into the winter and spoiled no faster than those that remained unscathed.

Deterring the woodchuck from further gastronomic pleasures at our expense was a more challenging endeavor, but one that was promptly solved by the use of a gas cartridge (prepared by the Pocatello Supply Depot, Pocatello, Idaho) which can be obtained through some hardware stores, including Agway. Woodchucks have a habit of tunneling under lush squash vegetation, and will dig a number of different entrances if allowed to do so. The trick is to locate each entrance and block up all but one with sod. The cartridge is ignited and placed as far into the open entrance as possible, followed by a clump of sod to seal in the gas and the woodchuck. The latter meets his maker and you enjoy the squash. To some readers, this procedure may appear heartless, yet it was either the woodchuck or the Halloween pumpkins! You may lose a squash plant or two because the gas may kill some roots, but this seems a small price to pay.

Other less desirable methods of ridding your garden of woodchucks, as well as raccoons, include wire traps in which the animal is taken alive (then disposed of on someone else's property) and the shotgun. The former can be exasperating if the animal is blessed with a modicum of intellect, and the latter is likely to raise the next-door neighbor's hackles, unless you live in a rural area where hunting and trapping are commonplace.

Birds

Scarecrows are the time-honored solution for deterring birds from enjoying your newly planted vegetable seeds. While they are great fun to make and attractive to look at if cleverly done, we have found them quite ineffective for "scaring the crows." Shiny, fluttering metal discs, which can be purchased from seed houses or garden supply stores, or simply tin can tops, strung across the garden in several places, do a better job. Pheasants find corn seeds particularly delicious in the spring, especially after we have fed them cracked corn all winter; however, they are encouraged to find their meals elsewhere by a barrage of glittering, clinking tin can tops. It is worth enduring the offense, both to eye and ear, for the short period of time it takes for the first planting of corn to germinate and take root. By the second and third plantings, the pheasants seem to be less enthusiastic about corn seeds, perhaps because food is more plentiful during June and July in the woods.

Insects and diseases

For many years we had little trouble from bugs or diseases. We did have potato bugs, we did have cutworms, and we did have damping-off with beets and carrots. These we could stand, but when some of the newer varieties of vegetables came on the market, we found additional troubles. With the hybrid varieties of corn came the corn borer and the earworm. Perhaps these would have come anyhow, but at least they appeared at the same time. Golden Delicious squash is particularly susceptible to the squash borer. Celery blight also made its appearance. Our garden procedure had not changed for years. We had used well-composted manure and fertilizers, mostly organic. When all the troubles appeared, something had to be done. We dislike the use of insecticides as much as anyone, but it was either insecticides or no garden.

In addition to the several insecticides we use, there are other steps the home gardener should follow to reduce or eliminate the destruction caused by insects and diseases. For example, we try to rotate our crops to a new location each year, thus making it unlikely that certain diseases will concentrate in any given area. When selecting new varieties, we lean toward those which have been found to be resistant to insects and diseases. Any vines or foliage that are heavily infested are removed at once and burned; they cannot be used for compost. Unfortunately, these steps have not proved as effective as we demand, with the result that additional precautions must be taken.

There are two schools of thought today — those who detest the use of poisonous sprays and those who are willing to use insecticides to save their gardens from the ravages of pests. If you are reluctant to spray or dust your vegetables with chemicals, there are dozens of other means that are said to deter insects, such as planting marigolds among certain vegetables to discourage nematodes. We have tried some, but our experience has been dismal at best. We might be faulted for not having given these methods a fair shake. In any event, we find it necessary to use several insecticides.

While there are dozens on the market, we confine ourselves to those insecticides that are readily available to the home gardener and relatively safe to use. The task of selecting the proper insecticide is made simpler if you stick to the all-purpose sprays, such as carbaryl, the trade name for which is Sevin. The secret of controlling pests is to use the designated insecticide before the pests arrive.

Our arsenal includes carbaryl (Sevin), malathion, methoxychlor, Diazinon, and rotenone. We have had difficulty with some pests and not others, so our spraying and dusting program may not necessarily be appropriate for your garden.

It is important to keep in mind the following when spraying:

1. Mix only enough for the immediate application.
2. Do not store diluted spray. The sediment at the bottom of the sprayer is difficult to remove once it has caked.
3. Keep all insecticides under lock and key.
4. Read and follow manufacturer's instructions with particular respect to the number of days to wait between application and harvest, the dilution table, and whether the product is designed

to eliminate the insect troubling you. It should be noted that some insecticides have a specific purpose and are utterly useless on pests other than those intended.

5. Never store herbicides near pesticides and fertilizers.

Here is a list of the insects that have bothered us:

Cutworms

They eat the plants of beans, beets, Brussels sprouts, cabbage, carrots, cauliflower, cucumbers, eggplant, limas, onions, spinach, squash, strawberry tomatoes, and tomatoes. Cutworms are eliminated by the use of Diazinon. We spray the soil before planting with a solution of 15 ounces, 25 percent Diazinon in enough water to cover 1000 square feet, usually 2 to 3 gallons. After the application, the soil is cultivated to a depth of 4 to 6 inches. We have also used chlordane in the past, and found it completely effective; we have now discontinued its use because it accumulates in the soil.

Cabbage worms

The plants of cabbage, Brussels sprouts, broccoli, and cauliflower are often damaged by these worms. They can be controlled by the use of carbaryl or malathion. If you see white butterflies, you can be sure infestation is on its way.

Corn borers and earworms

The corn borer eats the stalks. Whole rows can be devastated by these bugs, and the stalks will fall over, making a horrible mess. Bad as these are, the earworms are worse; there is something particularly repugnant about these slimy creatures. It is not pleasant to open ears of corn and find them inside. In our garden, these pests have never attacked the earliest corn, but on occasion they have done a great deal of damage to the midseason and late corn.

To prevent damage from the corn borer and the corn earworm,

we spray with carbaryl. For earworm, apply at fresh-silk stage to early and late corn every two days, four or five times. For the corn borer, apply four times every three days to whorl and ear zone.

Squash borers

Squash borers attack squash vines. These are miserable creatures. The moth lays the eggs near the base of the plants. When the eggs hatch, the borers emerge, enter the vine, and eat the insides. They kill the vines just when the latter are growing well. Within a few days, the borers can destroy practically all the squash plants. To control squash borers, spray the vines weekly with carbaryl or malathion.

Striped cucumber beetles

These are little black and yellow beetles that attack not only cucumbers but other vine crops. They are controlled if they are sprayed with either carbaryl or malathion.

Potato bugs

These bugs attack both potatoes and eggplant and are controlled by carbaryl or malathion.

Flea beetles

Flea beetles attack many garden plants and are destroyed by carbaryl.

Asparagus beetles

Asparagus beetles eat the asparagus plants and are controlled if sprayed with malathion, Sevin, or rotenone.

Mexican bean beetles

These beetles attack bush beans, pole beans, and limas. Our

GARDEN ENEMIES AND THE REMEDIES

Vegetable	Pest or disease	Insecticide or fungicide
Asparagus	Asparagus Beetle	Malathion, Carbaryl, Rotenone
Beans, Limas	Mexican Bean Beetle	Malathion, Carbaryl
Cabbage, Cauliflower, Broccoli, Brussels sprouts	Cabbage Worm	Malathion, Carbaryl
Carrots	Leaf Hopper	Carbaryl
	Carrot Rust Fly	Diazinon
Celery	Celery Blight	Maneb
	Aphids, Worms	Diazinon
Corn	Corn Borer	Carbaryl
	Corn Earworm	Carbaryl
	Seed Corn Maggot	Diazinon
Most garden crops (Beans, beets, Brussels sprouts, carrots, cauliflower, celery, cucumbers, eggplant, limas, onions, squash, strawberry tomatoes, tomatoes)	Cutworm	Diazinon, Carbaryl
	Flea Beetle	Carbaryl
Onions	Onion Maggot	Diazinon
Potatoes, Eggplant	Potato Bug	Carbaryl, Malathion
	Blight	Maneb
Cucumbers (Vine crops)	Cucumber Beetle	Carbaryl, Malathion
Squash	Squash Borer	Carbaryl, Malathion
Tomatoes	Blight and Insects	Ortho Tomato Vegetable Dust (combination insecticide and fungicide)

experience has been that they do not cause as much damage to the bush beans as to the pole beans, probably because the bush beans have a shorter growing season. We control them by applying either carbaryl or malathion to the foliage, paying particular attention to the underside of the leaves where the beetle does its work.

Blight

Maneb (Manzate) is an effective, all-purpose fungicide that may be used to control blight and other diseases on celery, potatoes, and tomatoes.

PREPARATION FOR WINTER

After the first fall frost there will be only a few vegetables surviving, such as broccoli, Brussels sprouts, beets, carrots, celery, fennel, and parsnips.* This is the time to start cleaning up the old foliage and adding it to the compost pile. The soil is easy to work in the fall, and this is when we plow in manure and compost. A cover crop, such as winter rye or annual rye, may be planted. There are several advantages to planting a cover crop, and one of the most important to us is that the garden looks lush and green during all but the dead of winter. A cover crop will also serve to improve the soil by adding nitrogen and building up organic matter. It will also reduce leaching and erosion.

* The main part of the garden will be finished and unattractive.

Cooking

You may well ask what cooking has to do with the raising of vegetables. The answer is "nothing." But cooking is a prime factor that will influence whether you can enjoy eating your good vegetables once you have grown them. How often we have seen really good vegetables absolutely ruined by poor cooking. Anyone who takes the trouble to raise vegetables should know how to cook them. It takes only very little practice to learn how to cook the few important ones, such as asparagus, beans, cauliflower, corn, and peas. The difference between poor cooking and good cooking is enormous, so, by all means, do a little thinking about cooking.

Our fundamental rules are simple and are as follows:

1. Cook as quickly as possible.

2. Don't cook vegetables ahead of time and let them stand. If you go to the trouble of raising good vegetables, it is far better that you wait a little for them than to have them wait for you.

3. Fancy sauces are not necessary.

4. Use the Mystery Chef Method for asparagus, beans, Brussels sprouts, cabbage, cauliflower, limas, peas, and spinach.

This method, described in *The Mystery Chef's Own Cook Book*, now available only in libraries, is briefly as follows: Fill and place two 3-quart size pots, one of which must be enamel, on the stove with the burners at the highest heat. When the water is boiling violently, add 1 teaspoon of baking soda to the enamel pot and 3 tablespoons of salt to the other pot. Add the vegetable to the pot with the baking soda and cook for 2 minutes, uncovered. Drain the water off and then add the boiling salt water to the vegetable and cook for 8 minutes, except as specified later. Drain and serve. The cabbage family — that is, cabbage, Brussels sprouts, and cauliflower — should be cooked for 3 minutes in the water with baking soda. The timing should be accurate, because overcooking in baking soda will ruin the taste; use a timer with a bell. And, wonder of wonders, there will be no odor of cooking cabbage.

Some people will say this two-pot method is a nuisance and won't use it. But if you want vegetables cooked to their best, this is the way to do it. Other people will say that the use of baking soda destroys the vitamins. The answer is that the vegetables are only partly cooked in the baking soda, just long enough to dissolve the unpleasant tasting impurities. Examine and smell the baking-soda solution after the first cooking. You will be surprised how unpleasant it is. According to some tests, the vitamins are not destroyed by cooking in baking soda for a short time. It is impossible to believe they could be, since this method of cooking produces vegetables of such superlative quality. Cooking by this method actually reduces the time of cooking (a great advantage), and the original color is retained. How much nicer it is to see the green vegetables, looking clean and sparkling, rather than a greenish brown, soggy mass.

Frozen green vegetables can be cooked by the same method, but the procedure is changed a little.

1. Don't take the frozen vegetables from the freezer until you are ready to use them.

2. When you are ready to start cooking, put the frozen vegetables in a pan of hot water for several minutes and stir occasionally. This will separate the frozen peas, or whatever you are using, and bring them up to approximately room temperature.

3. Use ½ teaspoon of baking soda in first treatment. Have the water boiling with the burner set at top speed. Cook the vegetables 2 minutes.

4. Drain, refill with the boiling salt water, and cook for 5 minutes.

The reason for using less time is that the vegetables were cooked a little when they were given the blanching treatment in boiling water (before they were frozen).

To obtain the maximum delicacy and flavor, asparagus, beans, and cauliflower should be served as a separate course, all by themselves, on toast, on very hot plates, with plenty of melted butter.

Regarding individual kinds, we offer these observations: broccoli, Brussels sprouts, and cabbage are generally held in low esteem, but when they are cooked by the baking-soda method they are delicious. They also have the advantage of being reasonably hardy. Brussels sprouts can be left in the garden and are excellent up to December 1, even after several frosts. If cooked au gratin, they are pretty good and certainly much better than the so-called fresh vegetables bought in the market at that time.

Cabbage, when shredded and cooked this way, is not only good to eat but beautiful to look at, since it has a very bright white and green coloration. Cabbage can be grown early in the spring and late in the fall; it should be used in those seasons, and not in the summer when there are other vegetables that can be grown only at that time.

Corn is the vegetable that receives the worst treatment of all. Generally, the poorer varieties are grown. Corn is kept for so many hours before it is used that nearly all the flavor is lost, and, finally, what little quality it has retained is destroyed by overcooking. It should be either dropped into a large pot of boiling water for only 3 minutes or cooked in a pressure cooker at 15 pounds for $1\frac{1}{2}$ minutes (from the time the pressure valve begins to sizzle).

For the green vegetables, if you prefer not to use the baking-soda method of cooking, then by all means use the pressure cooker. Asparagus, beans, limas, and peas that are young, tender, and freshly picked from the garden can be cooked in a pressure cooker set at 15 pounds in 2 minutes from the time the pressure valve begins to sizzle.

The parsnip is another vegetable with a poor reputation, but if it is cooked in the same way as julienne potatoes, you will think you are eating delicious sweet potatoes.

A wonderful combination is celery and milk. One improves the other. If you don't believe it, try for yourself.

Freezing and Storing

WE find it useful to freeze vegetables for the winter, and consider the quality of the home-frozen product well above the commercial frozen vegetable. Home freezing techniques were experimented with early at Candlewood and it was predicted correctly that quick-freezing would revolutionize the methods of keeping vegetables. Nowadays, many gardeners find it worth their time to fill a freezer with a large supply of their own vegetables to see them through the winter. It becomes increasingly important to be self-sufficient in these days of shortages. If you have a garden, and enjoy gardening and eating really good vegetables that will cause you to swell with pride when they appear on the table, then wild horses won't stop you from trying this adventure. But look upon it as a hobby as well as a practical means of obtaining good food, and plenty of it. One of the great advantages of the freezer is that all the vegetables are in condition for instant cooking; no shelling or washing is required. Simply take them out of the freezer, and put them in the pot. Because they are already partly cooked, it will take less time to cook them than fresh vegetables.

There is plenty of extra work involved if one is to savor the fruits of one's own summer labor throughout the winter. If you contemplate ordering a freezer and expect that the vegetables will meander in for processing all by themselves, then you had better leave well enough alone. Put the idea in the file labeled Don't Give It Another Thought. The vegetables must be picked in quantity, washed, shelled, or cut up, blanched, chilled, packaged, and carried to the freezer. It is a time-consuming operation, but once our family worked out the most effective technique it became a pleasant part of the summer routine. Because of current food shortages, each new addition to the freezer provides a relaxing sense of security. At Candlewood, it was carefully determined just how much of each vegetable would be needed through the winter, and the freezer was packed accordingly. For the use of two people during the five winter months of November, December, January, February, and March, the following amounts were frozen:

Asparagus	40 pints
Limas	40 pints
Peas	30 pints
Corn	30 packages (3 ears each)

At Craigston, we simply freeze as much of everything as we possibly can, and there's never anything left by asparagus season except a few unsuccessful experiments. Don't allow this task to rest solely on the lady of the house. It is a big job and is most efficiently accomplished if the whole family contributes time to it. Little children make very good pea shellers, but be sure to feed them well before they start or they'll eat most of the harvest. We find the best system for us is to pick in the late afternoon and prepare the vegetables for the freezer in the cool and peace of the evening, with all hands present. It is vitally important to allow as little time as possible between harvesting and freezing. For instance, it takes months for corn to acquire its superb flavor, but only minutes to lose it! If you are unable to begin freezing shortly after harvesting, the produce should be kept in the refrigerator.

Some vegetables freeze better than others, and often one variety of a certain vegetable freezes better than another. As a rule of thumb, the varieties with the more pronounced taste are best for freezing. They are more apt to retain their flavor through the blanching process. Also, the darker the color of the vegetable, the stronger the taste. This is perhaps best illustrated by comparing summer squash with beets. The seed catalogs, particularly Harris', usually provide a good indication of which variety one should choose for freezing purposes, and we have found the advice reliable. However, it is better to use what grows best in your garden rather than something that does not grow so well, although it might be better for freezing.

We freeze the following vegetables: asparagus, beans, beets (only if we can't eat them all by the time they are the size of Ping-Pong balls), broccoli, cauliflower, corn, limas, peas, prepared winter squash, and tomatoes in the form of sauce or soup. We usually eat all the carrots in the summer and buy them very reasonably in the winter, but if you should have an excess, it can be frozen for use in stews. In all our experiments at Craigston, the frozen carrots end up limp and soggy. Soups can be made from zucchini, beets (if by mistake they are allowed to reach their mature size), and cucumbers, and then frozen successfully. Raspberries, strawberries, and rhubarb may be frozen for use in desserts. The berries should not, however, be used with cream as if they were fresh. When thawed, they are soft and mushy.

Of all the herbs we grow, the ones we use the most are mint for lamb; tarragon for steaks, eggs, and salads; and chives for salads. What a pleasure it is, in midwinter when the ground is covered with snow, to have home-grown tarragon on your steak or mint sauce on your lamb. If you like herbs, you will find that freezing them for winter use is well-expended effort.

We have experimented with all the vegetables we grow and have found only potatoes and summer squash to be unfreezable in any form. It is our opinion that summer squash, while easy to grow, cannot compare with most other vegetables. Who would opt for this virtually tasteless and colorless vegetable when offered corn, peas, or asparagus as an alternative? It is barely acceptable when smothered and disguised with generous doses of soured cream and seasoned salt.

THE PROCEDURE FOR FREEZING

1. *Use only vegetables and fruits of the highest quality.*
Remember that you will take out just what you put in, and,
unfortunately, freezing does not have the magic quality of
improving vegetables. It often seems as if people want to
believe, because they have taken a little trouble, that vegetables
so stored will suddenly assume all the qualities they desire. That
is far from the case. It is necessary to use twice as much care in
selecting good vegetables for freezing as it is to select vegetables
from the garden to be cooked and eaten as soon as they are
picked. Vegetables grown in the early season and picked just
when they are ripe are those best-suited for freezing. In particular, use early peas and corn for freezing. The early maturing
varieties are much better than those that mature later.

In summer, home-grown vegetables certainly can be much
better than those bought in stores. So-called fresh peas, string
beans, and other kinds bought from stores in winter are much
poorer than those bought in summer. If home-grown vegetables
can be frozen in summer, they will certainly be better than those
bought fresh in winter.

2. *Pick at the right moment.* Don't freeze anything you
wouldn't enjoy eating the moment it was picked. With most
vegetables, it is best to freeze them on the young side, and yet
you must be careful to wait until they are mature enough to
produce their utmost in quantity without sacrificing quality.
Baby peas are delicious, but large, old peas aren't worth eating.
There seems to be an intermediate stage that is best for freezing.
It takes a lot of tiny peas to provide enough for a meal and it is
decidedly worthwhile to be extravagant in your allowances.

3. *Wash in cold water and prepare as you would for the table.*
The harvest should be cleaned thoroughly in either cold running
water or ice water. There is nothing as unappetizing as biting
into a mouthful of spinach laced with sand or broccoli adorned

with worms. If you are confident of the procedures you use for ridding the broccoli of cabbage worms, there is no need for the following. Otherwise, broccoli should be left in a bowl of salt water (1 tablespoon per quart) for an hour or so, after which the worms will have been separated from their feast. They are difficult to detect in the buds and generally can be seen only from the stem end.

Keep in mind that one can alleviate boredom with winter meals by using a variety of methods of preparation. At Craigston, we freeze beans whole, cut up in ¼-inch slices, and cut lengthwise. Broccoli, beets, and spinach may be either chopped or left whole, as dictated by one's whim. The children love everything whole, particularly beans and broccoli (which they call "trees").

4. *Blanch.* The process of boiling or steaming the vegetables in order to stop the action of enzymes preserves the characteristics of freshness. It seems that enzymes act to break down the tissues of the vegetables, and this results in increasingly inferior texture, color, and flavor. Their work ceases at the boiling point. The alternative — that is, freezing without blanching — produces results similar to what is found after a fall frost. The nonhardy vegetables left in the garden are shriveled, wilted, and tasteless.

Fill a large kettle three-fourths full and bring it to a rapid, rolling boil. Put a smallish amount of the vegetable in a mesh basket or cheesecloth (good for peas or cut beans, which go through the basket) and plunge it in the boiling water. Start timing when the water returns to a boil. You must adjust the amount of vegetables so that the water resumes boiling quickly, within two minutes. Speed is an important factor, otherwise you will end up with soggy vegetables. Use a kitchen timer with a bell, or simply watch the clock. Blanching times are given in a chart at the end of this chapter. As you become more experienced, you will simply know when the vegetable is ready.

Also, after a few sessions, you will find that you are able to keep two or three pots going at once, an act similar to a circus juggler's.

5. *Chill.* Lift the vegetables out of the boiling water and plunge them into ice water in order to stop the cooking process as fast as possible. At Craigston, we use the kitchen sink for this purpose. Large blocks of ice, made by freezing water in milk cartons or coffee cans, are the most effective way to keep the water chilled. Remember that it takes as long to bring the vegetables back to 50 or 60 degrees as it did to raise them to 212 degrees.

6. *Drain and dry the vegetables.* We lay the chilled vegetables on terry-cloth towels, which must be changed frequently; have a dry supply ready. If extra quick freezing is desired, lay the vegetables in a single layer on cookie sheets and put them in the freezer for half an hour and then package. The quicker the freezing point is reached, the better the results, but this is a time-consuming technique and we feel it is necessary only with corn because the cob retains the heat a long time even with the ice-water bath.

7. *Package.* Plastic freezer boxes of various sizes can be bought for peas, cut-up beans, and spinach; plastic bags can be used for the more unwieldy vegetables, such as corn, broccoli, and uncut beans. If you use cartons, leave about $\frac{1}{4}$ inch headroom, and if you use bags, try to squeeze all the air out. Package in a variety of sizes: children's meals, family meals, party meals.

8. *Freeze.* When we first put the produce in the freezer, the packages are distributed in various locations so that they will freeze faster. They are put in their final resting places the next day. A grouping of unfrozen packages will take much longer to freeze than a single one.

We consider meticulous labeling a waste of time if you arrange your vegetables in groups in the freezer, for example, putting beans in the upper right-hand corner every year. Of course, mashed Hubbard squash and mashed pumpkin must be labeled because of the similarity of their appearance, but what could be more fun than opening a package of peas and finding the last of the blueberries for a February pie?

We consider it important to empty the freezer of vegetables every spring before adding the new season's harvest; there are always friends who will be thrilled with a few packages of home-frozen beans. We find that the quality definitely deteriorates after a year's time.

The procedure for freezing herbs is very simple. Wash and clean the herbs, cut off the stems and poor leaves, package in foil in amounts you would use at one time, put the packages of each variety in their own plastic bag. Blanching is unnecessary for herbs, and is not needed for blueberries, raspberries, rhubarb, and peppers (for use in cooking, because they lose their crispness).

The following table shows the area required and also the time required for picking, preparing, and freezing.

Vegetable	*Pints wanted*	*Feet of row to produce 1 pint*	*Total footage of rows*	*Hours required for picking*	*Hours required for freezing*	*Hours total*	*Hours per pint*
Asparagus	40	5	200	4	11	15	0.4
Corn (packages)	30	2.5	76	2	4	6	.2
Limas	40	2	80	7	13	20	.5
Peas	30	1.5	46	5	12	17	.6
Raspberries	20	2	40	5	2	7	.3
Strawberries	16	1.5	24	5	2	7	.5
Rhubarb	16		19	2	2	4	.3
Peaches	20			2	2	4	.2
Totals	212		485	32	48	80	

4 plants will produce the rhubarb.
1 tree will produce the peaches.

STORING

Some vegetables can be stored successfully without freezing. At Craigston, we keep Acorn, Butternut and Blue Hubbard squash in a little unheated room in the cellar until about March 1. We make a point of eating the acorn first, because it is our experience that it doesn't keep quite as well as the others. Also, it's our favorite! The ideal temperature for cold storage is between 35 and 40 degrees. It is mandatory to keep the produce from freezing and it is best to provide some kind of ventilation. The stored vegetables should be kept in a single layer so that they will not touch one another.

At Candlewood, celery and parsnips are picked through the fall and winter and may be left in the ground until January 1 and March 1, respectively. These two vegetables are protected by a covering of salt straw or hay and by corrugated steel roofing sheets placed over that. Even snow (unless it is deeper than 6 inches) or a cold spell does not prevent us from picking them. It is easy to slide the metal sheet along and uncover as much of the vegetables as we want. We find this method easier and better than harvesting and storing them.

As far as storing root crops is concerned, it is our belief that stored beets and carrots do not make good eating. They just get poorer and poorer and we hate even to look at them. Potatoes can be stored successfuly, but why bother; their brothers in the market are generally of better or equal quality, and we defy anyone to discern between a home-grown baking potato stored until midwinter and one purchased in the market.

We keep vegetables for winter use by one of the methods shown in the chart opposite.

At Craigston, we do no canning or processing because we have found freezing to be entirely satisfactory. It is certainly a much simpler operation, the quality is far superior, and there are no worries about botulism. We do, however, make pickles and relishes of various descriptions, which are put up in Ball jars.

	Storing in ground	Storing in cold cellar	Processing	Freezing
Asparagus				X
Beets			X	
Carrots			X	
Celery	X			
Corn				X
Limas				X
Onions, Yellow Globe		X		
Onions, Shallots		X		
Parsnips	X			
Peas				X
Potatoes		X		
Squash		X		

An extremely useful publication, *Complete Guide to Home Canning, Preserving, and Freezing*, has recently been assembled by the United States Department of Agriculture (Dover Publications, 1973). We have found this a thorough guide and a useful kitchen reference.

APPENDIX A

Seed Lists and Planting Dates

THIS part has to do only with lists and dates, uninteresting but important. If you have a good garden and are interested in it, keep yearly records, particularly of what and when you plant and when each crop matures. Although there are many excellent gardens for which no records are kept and the gardener's memory is the record book, we feel that there are a considerable number of advantages to be gained if someone takes the trouble to keep records.

SEED LIST FOR GARDEN

Vegetable	Feet of row	Amt.	Variety	Source
Asparagus			Waltham Washington	Seedway
Beans	494	2 lbs.	Topcrop	Burpee
Beets (Early)	190	2 oz.	Ruby Queen	Harris
Beets (Late)	114	2 oz.	Red Ball	Burpee
Brussels Sprouts	38	1 pkt.	Catskill	Harris
Carrots	266	3 oz.	Nantes	Harris
Cauliflower (Early)	20	1 pkt.	Snowball	Harris
Cauliflower (Late)	152	½ oz.	Purple Head	Harris
Celery	152	2 pkt.	Summer Pascal (Tall Fordhook)	Burpee
Corn (Earliest)	266	1 lb.	Seneca 60	Robson
Corn (Early)	114	½ lb.	Sugar and Gold	Agway
Corn (Main Crop)	228	1 lb.	Seneca Chief	Robson

continued on next page

Vegetable	Feet of row	Amt.	Variety	Source
Cucumbers, 5 plants		1 pkt.	Marketer	Burpee
Eggplant, 9 plants		1 pkt.	Jersey King	Burpee
Fennel	76	1 oz.	Florence	Burpee
Jerusalem Artichoke	25	2 qts.	Jerusalem Artichoke	Park
Leeks	76	2 pkts.	Musselburgh	Unwins
Lettuce (Early)	228	2 pkts.	May King	Chase
Lettuce	494	3 pkts.	Buttercrunch	Burpee
Limas	228	2 lbs.	Fordhook 242	Burpee
Onions	76	½ oz.	White Queen	Vilmorin
Onions	152	½ oz.	Danvers Yellow Globe	Hart
Onions	38	½ oz.	Japanese Bunching	Harris
Onions	152	3 lbs.	Shallots	Gurney
Parsnips	38	1 oz.	All American	Harris
Peas (Frame)	76	2½ lbs.	Alaska	Burpee
Peas (Earliest)	38	1¼ lbs.	World's Record	Hart
Peas (Main Crop)	152	5 lbs.	Victory Freezer	Unwins
Peas (Latest)	152	5 lbs.	Lincoln	Harris
Potatoes	76	1 peck	Irish Cobbler	Agway
Potatoes	76	1 peck	Green Mountain	Agway
Radishes	76	2 oz.	Champion	Harris
Rhubarb, 6 plants			Valentine	Burpee
Spinach	190	¼ lb.	America	Burpee
Squash, 4 hills		2 pkts.	Golden Delicious	Harris
Tomatoes		1 pkt.	Strawberry Husk	Burpee
Tomatoes, 3 plants		1 pkt.	Red Cherry	Burpee
Tomatoes, 16 plants		1 pkt.	Moreton Hybrid	Harris

Most of the early vegetables planted in the northern half of the middle and eastern United States would be planted within the time limits of the following table:

	Delaware (Newark)	Ohio (Columbus)	Mass. (Ipswich)	New York (Ithaca)
Last frost	Apr. 19	May 6	May 12	May 20
First planting				
Peas	Mar. 20	Apr. 1	Mar. 29	Apr. 1
Beans	Apr. 15	May 1	Apr. 15	May 15
Corn	Apr. 15	May 15	May 1	May 15
Limas	May 5	May 20	June 1	May 25

Obtain the average date of the last killing frost in your vicinity, (see chart, pages 206–207) and then draw up your own planting schedule, using the above dates for the first plantings. The last planting of quick-maturing corn should be ninety days before the first frost and the last planting of beans seventy days.

PLANTING SCHEDULE — GREENHOUSE

Predicated on Ipswich planting dates. Adjust for your own region.

Sow	Vegetable	Variety
Feb. 20	Beets	Ruby Queen
20	Cauliflower	Snowball
20	Leeks	Musselburgh
20	Lettuce	May King
20	Onions	Japanese Bunching
20	Onions	Danvers Yellow Globe
Mar. 1	Eggplant	Jersey King
15	Celery	Summer Pascal (Tall Fordhook)
15	Lettuce	May King
15	Tomatoes	Red Cherry
15	Tomatoes	Strawberry Husk

continued on next page

PLANTING SCHEDULE — GREENHOUSE (*continued*)

Predicated on Ipswich planting dates. Adjust for your own region.

Sow		Vegetable	Variety
	15	Tomatoes	Moreton Hybrid
	31	Lettuce	Buttercrunch
Apr.	5	Onions	Danvers Yellow Globe
	12	Lettuce	Buttercrunch
	22	Lettuce	Buttercrunch
May	1	Lettuce	Buttercrunch
	5	Brussels sprouts	Catskill
	7	Lettuce	Buttercrunch
	14	Lettuce	Buttercrunch
	21	Lettuce	Buttercrunch
	28	Lettuce	Buttercrunch
June	8	Lettuce	Buttercrunch
	15	Lettuce	Buttercrunch
	23	Lettuce	Buttercrunch
July	2	Lettuce	Buttercrunch
	12	Lettuce	Buttercrunch
	20	Lettuce	May King
Aug.	1	Lettuce	May King
	8	Lettuce	May King

PLANTING SCHEDULE — GARDEN

Predicated on Ipswich planting dates. Adjust for your own region.

Sow	Vegetable	Variety
Mar. 18	Peas	Alaska, Frame
29	Peas	World's Record
29	Peas	Victory Freezer
Apr. 1	T. Lettuce	May King, Frame
1	Parsnip	All American

Letter T. preceding a vegetable indicates a transplanted seedling.

PLANTING SCHEDULE — GARDEN (*continued*)

Predicated on Ipswich planting dates. Adjust for your own region.

Sow		Vegetable	Variety
	1	Spinach	America
	1	Cauliflower	Purple Head
	10	Onion Sets	Shallots
	10	Spinach	America
	15	Beans	Topcrop
	15	Beets	Ruby Queen
	15	Carrots	Nantes
	15	T. Lettuce	May King
	15	Radishes	Champion
	15	Jerusalem Artichokes	Jerusalem Artichoke
	21	Peas	Lincoln
	22	Corn	Seneca 60, Frame
	25	Radishes	Champion
May	1	Potatoes	Green Mountain
	1	Beets	Ruby Queen
	1	Carrots	Nantes
	1	Corn	Seneca 60
	1	Cucumbers	Marketer
	1	Leeks	Musselburgh
	1	Onions	Danvers Yellow Globe
	1	Onions ⅔ row	Japanese Bunching
	1	Onions	White Queen
	1	Potatoes	Irish Cobbler
	5	Radishes	Champion
	6	T. Lettuce	Buttercrunch
	6	Peas	Lincoln
May	8	Cauliflower	Purple Head
	9	Beets	Ruby Queen
	12	Beans	Topcrop
	14	Peas	Lincoln
	15	Corn	Sugar and Gold

Letter T. preceding a vegetable indicates a transplanted seedling.

continued on next page

PLANTING SCHEDULE — GARDEN (*continued*)
Predicated on Ipswich planting dates. Adjust for your own region.

Sow		Vegetable	Variety
	15	Radishes	Champion
	16	T. Lettuce	Buttercrunch
	16	Onions ⅛ row	Japanese Bunching
	18	Peas	Lincoln
	18	Potatoes	Irish Cobbler
	24	Cauliflower	Purple Head
	25	Cucumbers	Marketer
	25	T. Lettuce	Buttercrunch
	25	Radishes	Champion
	27	Corn	Seneca Chief
	29	Corn	Sugar and Gold
	30	Beans	Topcrop
June	1	T. Celery	Summer Pascal (Tall Fordhook)
	1	T. Eggplant	Jersey King
	1	Limas	Fordhook 242
	1	Squash	Golden Delicious
	1	T. Tomatoes	Red Cherry
	1	T. Tomatoes	Moreton Hybrid
	1	Cucumbers	Marketer
	4	T. Lettuce	Buttercrunch
	4	Cauliflower	Purple Head
	5	Radishes	Champion
	6	Onions ⅛ row	Japanese Bunching
	6	Fennel	Florence
	7	Beets	Red Ball
	8	Corn	Seneca Chief
June	10	Onions	Danvers Yellow Globe
	10	Carrots	Nantes
	10	Corn	Sugar and Gold
	12	T. Lettuce	Buttercrunch
	12	T. Tomatoes	Strawberry Husk

Letter T. preceding a vegetable indicates a transplanted seedling.

PLANTING SCHEDULE — GARDEN (*continued*)

Predicated on Ipswich planting dates. Adjust for your own region.

Sow		Vegetable	Variety
	14	Beans	Topcrop
	15	Radishes	Champion
	17	Corn	Seneca Chief
	20	Brussels sprouts	Catskill
	22	T. Lettuce	Buttercrunch
	24	Corn	Seneca Chief
	25	Beans	Topcrop
	25	Radishes	Champion
	27	Beets	Red Ball
	28	Corn	Seneca Chief
	29	T. Lettuce	Buttercrunch
July	3	Corn	Seneca 60
	5	Beans	Topcrop
	5	T. Lettuce	Buttercrunch
	5	Radishes	Champion
	8	Carrots	Nantes
	9	Beets	Red Ball
	9	Onions ⅓ row	Japanese Bunching
	11	Corn	Seneca 60
	14	Beans	Topcrop
	15	T. Lettuce	Buttercrunch
	15	Radishes	Champion
	16	Carrots	Nantes
	24	Beans	Topcrop
	24	T. Lettuce	Buttercrunch
	25	Radishes	Champion
Aug.	1	Beans	Topcrop
	3	T. Lettuce	Buttercrunch
	5	Radishes	Champion
	7	Beans	Topcrop

Letter T. preceding a vegetable indicates a transplanted seedling.

continued on next page

PLANTING SCHEDULE — GARDEN *(continued)*

Predicated on Ipswich planting dates. Adjust for your own region.

Sow	Vegetable	Variety
8	Beans	Topcrop, Frame
12	T. Lettuce	Buttercrunch
14	Beans	Topcrop, Frame
15	Radishes	Champion
23	T. Lettuce	Buttercrunch
25	Radishes	Champion
29	T. Lettuce	May King, Frame
29	T. Lettuce	Buttercrunch, Frame
Sept. 5	Radishes	Champion
10	T. Lettuce	May King, Frame
15	Radishes	Champion
18	T. Lettuce	May King, Frame
25	Radishes	Champion

Letter T. preceding a vegetable indicates a transplanted seedling.

PLANTING SCHEDULE — HOTFRAMES — SPRING AND FALL[*]

Transplant to frame	Plant in frame	Vegetable	Variety
Mar. 25		Lettuce	May King
	Apr. 1	Radishes	Champion
Apr. 1		Beets	Ruby Queen
1		Cauliflower	Snowball
Aug. 29		Lettuce	May King
Sept. 10		Lettuce	May King
18		Lettuce	May King

[*] While vegetables are planted in the hotframes in the fall, no heat is used. The frames are actually run as coldframes.

MATERIAL REQUIRED

Poles: ¾-in. bamboo painted green

For	Length of poles (ft.)	Spaced	Total
Tomatoes — 1 row	6	3 every 24 in.	60
Brussels sprouts — 1 row	4	1 every 30 in.	15
Eggplant — ½ row	3	1 every 30 in.	8

Pipe: 1-in. galvanized painted green

For	Length of pipe (ft.)	Spaced	Total
Around garden	4	1 every 12 ft.	according to size
Brussels sprouts — 1 row	6	1 every 19 ft.	3
Eggplant — ½ row	5	1 every 10 ft.	2
Peas — 11 rows	6	1 every 10 ft.	50
Tomatoes — 1 row	7	1 every 19 ft.	3

Wire Mesh

For	Mesh size (in.)	Spaced	Total
Peas — 4-ft. chicken wire	2	11 rows	418 ft.
Rabbits — 30-in. close woven	½	around garden	according to size

Wire: 10-gauge galvanized

For	Length of rows (ft.)
Brussels sprouts	40
Corn	160
Eggplant	20
Tomatoes	40
Total:	260

String: 10 balls soft jute twine can be used many times

Paint: Moore's Arbor Green, No. 21

continued on page 210

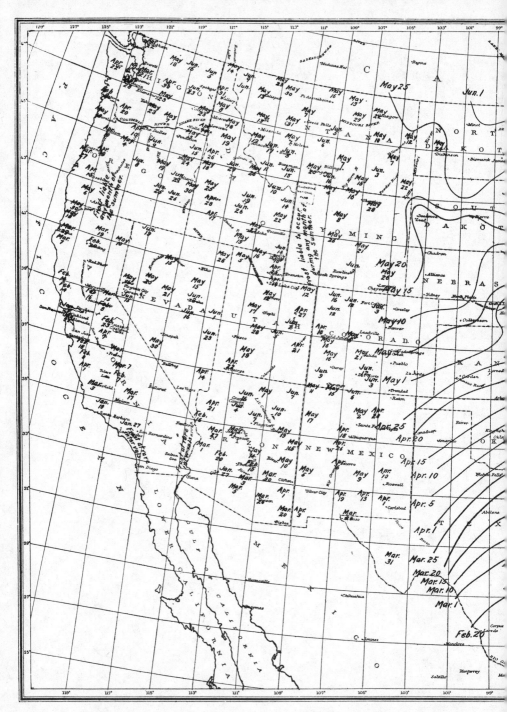

THE AVERAGE DATE OF THE LAST KILLING FROST IN SPRING

Plant vegetables at such dates that they will not be killed by the last frost.

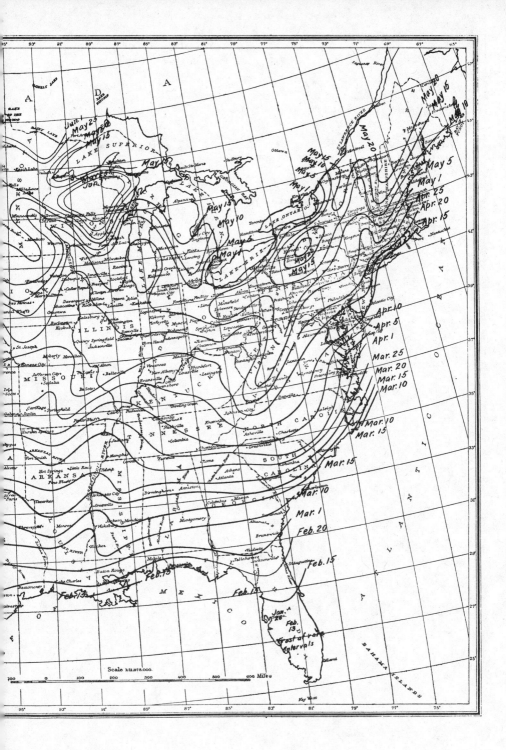

continued from page 207.

Mulch: Baled Salt Hay

Fertilizers

Manure	0–20–20	Superphosphate
5–10–10	13–26–13	Limestone

Insecticides, Fungicides and Herbicides

Methoxychlor	Rotenone	Maneb
Sevin	Diazinon	Pyrethrins
Malathion	Captan	

The Weekend Garden

THE weekend garden is for those who would like to have a vegetable garden that requires the minimum amount of time with the maximum results, and one that can be worked on at convenient times. All dates given are for weekends in 1972. For later years, use nearest weekend.

WEEKEND, MINIMUM-EFFORT VEGETABLE GARDEN

This garden, 25 x 51 feet, is designed to produce the maximum amount of vegetables with the minimum amount of work. It has been used for several seasons and is not in any way an experiment. The land for this garden was used the previous year so that it was in good condition. During the last season this garden produced by actual weight and count the following crops:

Vegetable	Variety	Source	Amt.	Approx. cost	No. rows	Total feet	Produced ears, heads	lbs.
Beans	Topcrop	Burpee	3 lbs.	$4.65	11	275		89
Beets (early)	Ruby Queen	Harris	1 oz.	.80	2	50		50
Beets (late)	Red Ball	Burpee	½ oz.	.50	1	25		25
Broccoli	Waltham 29	Harris	1 pkt.	.35	1	25		25

continued on next page

Vegetable	Variety	Source	Amt.	Approx. cost	No. rows	Total feet	Produced ears, heads	lbs.
Carrots	Nantes	Harris	½ oz.	.50	3	75		40
Corn (early)	Sugar and Gold	Agway	½ lb.	1.00	2	50	40	
Corn (late)	Seneca 60	Robson	½ lb.	1.00	4	125	140	
Lettuce	White Boston	Burpee	1 pkt.	.35	1	25	30	
Lettuce	Great Lakes	Harris	1 pkt.	.40	1	25	30	
Limas	King of the Garden	Harris	1 pkt.	.35	1	25		
Parsnips	All America	Harris	1 pkt.	.30	2	50		90
Peas	Greater Progress	Harris	2 lbs.	2.90	3	75		20
Peas	Lincoln	Harris	2 lbs.	2.90	3	75		30
Radishes	Champion	Harris	1 oz.	.70	2	50		
Spinach	America	Burpee	1 oz.	.45	2	50		25
Tomatoes	Moreton Hybrid	Harris	1 pkt.	.55	2	50		72
			Totals	$17.70	41		240	466

Seedlings to be started indoors and transplanted to garden

Broccoli	16	18 in. apart in row
Lettuce	60	10 in. apart in row
Tomatoes	14	4 ft. apart in row

Addresses

Robson Seed Farm, Hall, N.Y. 14463
Joseph Harris Co., Rochester, N.Y. 14624
W. Atlee Burpee Co., Philadelphia, Pa. 19132
Agway, Box 1333, Syracuse, N.Y. 13201

It took a skilled professional gardener 26¼ hours to look after

Plant in garden		Vegetable	Variety	Set plants in garden	Mature	Finish
April	1	Spinach			May 24	June 15
	1	Peas	Greater Progress		June 21	June 27
	1	Parsnips			Oct. 1	Mar. 10
	15	Radishes			May 18	June 1
	15	Beets	Ruby Queen		June 15	July 25
	15	Carrots			June 25	July 25
	15	Peas	Greater Progress		June 26	July 2
	15	Beans			July 2	July 12
	29	Peas	Victory Freezer		July 1	July 6
	29	Beans			July 4	July 14
	29	Radishes			June 1	June 11
		Lettuce		April 29	June 10	June 20
	29	Carrots			July 10	Aug. 15
May	6	Beets	Ruby Queen		June 28	Aug. 28
	6	Beans			July 7	July 17
	6	Peas	Victory Freezer		July 11	July 17
	8	Radishes			June 10	June 20
		Lettuce		May 14	June 20	June 30
		Broccoli		May 20	July 10	July 30
	20	Corn	Sugar and Gold		Aug. 2	Aug. 10
	20	Limas			Aug. 27	Oct. 1
	20	Radishes			June 25	July 5
		Lettuce		May 27	July 3	July 12
		Tomatoes		June 3	July 20	Oct. 10
	27	Beans			July 25	Aug. 4
June	9	Corn	Seneca 60		Aug. 19	Aug. 25
	17	Corn	Seneca 60		Aug. 25	Sept. 1
	17	Radishes			July 15	July 25
		Lettuce		June 17	July 15	July 25
July	1	Corn	Seneca 60		Sept. 8	Sept. 15
	1	Radishes			Aug. 1	Aug. 11
		Lettuce		July 1	Aug. 1	Aug. 11
	1	Beans			Aug. 18	Aug. 28
	1	Carrots			Aug. 25	Dec. 1
	1	Beets	Red Ball		Sept. 10	Dec. 1
	1	Radishes			Aug. 8	Aug. 25
		Lettuce		July 8	Aug. 15	Aug. 25
	8	Beans			Aug. 25	Sept. 3
	15	Beans			Sept. 4	Sept. 14
	22	Beans			Sept. 14	Sept. 24

All planting dates are on weekends for 1972. For other years change nearest weekend.

Distance between rows in feet	PRIOR CROP Plant	PRIOR CROP Vegetable	SECOND STORY CROP Vegetable	SECOND STORY CROP Plant	FOLLOW CROP Vegetable	FOLLOW CROP Plant
1	April 1	Spinach	Tomatoes	June 3	Beets Red Ball	July 1
2	1	Spinach			Carrots	1
1	1	Parsnips	Tomatoes	June 3		
2	1	Beans				
2	15	Parsnips			Beans	22
2	1	Beets R.Q.	and Corn S.G.	April 29		
2	15	Peas G.P.	and Corn S60	May 20	Beans	1
2	15	Carrots	and Corn S60	June 9	Beans	7
2	15	Peas G.P.	and Corn S60	June 9	Beans	15
2	29	Carrots			Support on wire	
2	15	Peas G.P.				
2	29	Beans L.				
2	29	Beets				
2	May 6	Beans R.Q.			Support on wire	
2	6	Peas L.	Corn S60	June 17		
2	6	Peas L.	Corn S60	July 1	Support on wire	
2	6	Broccoli				
2	20	Beans	Limas	May 20		
2	May 27	Lettuce W.B.				
1	April 29*	Lettuce G.L.				
1	June 17*	Radishes			Radish	
1	April 15*					

Make 3 Plantings ⅓ row each time
Make 3 Plantings ⅓ row each time
Make 7 Plantings ¼ row each time

51' Length

25' Width

N / S / E / W

*First Planting Date

this garden for the entire season, including the time for preparing the soil in the spring and the time for cleaning up the garden in the fall. The time required to pick the vegetables is not included.

The time required by others will be in proportion to their skill and strength. This garden can provide enough fresh summer vegetables for a family of four.

	(*Hrs.*)
April	4
May	3
June	10
July	5
August	2
September	2¼
Total:	26¼

In regard to the garden design, most people will agree that, except for asparagus, which comes from a permanent bed, corn, peas, and beans are the most popular vegetables. It is impossible to buy in the markets these vegetables of a quality anywhere near that which can be achieved by growing them in the home garden. The garden plan was designed to grow these vegetables with the highest quality, a few other vegetables that mature very early in the spring, and a few late vegetables. This program provides for a long season of production. Many people advise against planting peas and corn, because they take up so much room, but if they are grown in the manner suggested, they are simply additional crops on ground already planted. Personally, we can't imagine a home garden without them. To plant such vegetables as chard, peppers, potatoes, spinach, summer squash, and onions for winter, all of which can be bought of good quality in the markets, seems to us to be nonsense. The varieties selected are those that have been proved, by tests, to do best in this type of garden. To obtain the maximum sunlight, the rows should run north and south.

If you would like to reduce the garden size and still grow the most desirable varieties, eliminate the rows of broccoli and parsnips. This will make the garden 45 x 25 feet and reduce the hours of labor by one-seventh. If you want a still smaller garden, reduce the width but do not reduce the length.

Two varieties of beets are recommended: Ruby Queen for early, and Red Ball for late. The latter variety is the only kind we have found of which late plantings were almost as good as early sowings.

Corn in two varieties is planted: Sugar and Gold for early, and Seneca 60 for late. Sugar and Gold will not germinate well if planted earlier than May 20. This variety is low-growing, and its shade will not hurt the other low-growing crops if it is planted in hills 4 feet apart in the rows that have had prior crops. Put four seeds of corn in each hill. Two of the seeds should be on one side and two on the other side of the prior crop row. Because of shade difficulties, the last 2 rows of corn have no prior crops and the hills should be planted 2 feet apart.

Parsnips are not popular with most people, but if cooked exactly like julienne potatoes, they are really delicious. They can be covered in the late fall, left in the garden all winter, and picked whenever you want them. If you won't have parsnips, plant anything you like better in the 2 rows allowed.

Peas of two varieties are included: for early, Greater Progress, which is a dwarf pea that needs no support, and Lincoln, for late. The latter variety grows 30 inches tall and needs support, which can be chicken wire tied to pipes set in the row. As the pea vines grow, they should be tied to the wire by long loops of string. Tomatoes are staked; the poles for the plants are set 4 feet apart in the rows. Set the tomato plants on one side of the poles.

For humus, use one-third of a cord of garden compost or manure. If neither can be obtained, use dried manure, which can be bought at garden supply stores. For fertilizer, use seventy-five pounds of 5–10–10 garden fertilizer; fifty pounds should be broadcast in the spring and raked in and twenty pounds should be used on the follow crops, with five pounds in the pea rows.

For mulch, use baled salt-marsh hay over the garden. Let the plants grow 4 or 5 inches, weed once, and then spread the hay 5 inches thick. No more weeding will be required all summer, and the ground will not dry out. In a drought, the use of salt hay as a mulch is invaluable. If you can't buy salt hay, use baled peat moss.

To prevent damage by rabbits, set pipes upright along the garden edges and tie 30-inch chicken wire to the pipes. Bury 5 inches of wire in the ground and there will be no more rabbit trouble in the garden.

To obtain almost perfect germination, dust the pea, bean, and parsnip seed with captan, which can be bought at some seed houses.

To obtain top results on broccoli and tomatoes, scoop out a hole where the plants are to be set, and mix into each hole a handful of good garden compost. Failing that, make up a mixture of one part Bovung, one part peat moss, and one-half part bone meal.

The following insecticides are recommended:

Use Sevin (carbaryl) or Diazinon for soil treatment before planting in early spring to kill cutworms.

Use Sevin, following label instructions, on beans, limas, broccoli, carrots, corn, and tomatoes to eliminate flea beetles, Mexican bean beetles, cabbage worms, corn borers, and corn earworms.

Index